Editor
Melissa Hart, M.F.A.

Managing Editor
Ina Massler Levin, M.A.

Editor-in-Chief
Sharon Coan, M.S. Ed.

Illustrator
Sue Fullam

Cover Artist
Brenda DiAntonis

Art Coordinator
Kevin Barnes

Imaging
Rosa C. See

Product Manager
Phil Garcia

Publisher
Mary D. Smith, M.S. Ed.

S0-BRV-341

EXPANDING
The Writing Process
with
Elaboration
Grades 5 & Up

VIVID

Fluttering

EFFERVESCENT

Brilliant

Challenging

Written by

Joyce Caskey

Teacher Created Resources

Teacher Created Resources, Inc.
6421 Industry Way
Westminster, CA 92683
www.teachercreated.com

ISBN 13: 978-0-7439-3629-3

©2002 Teacher Created Resources, Inc.
Reprinted, 2007
Made in U.S.A.

Table of Contents

Introduction to Teachers

Developing ideas for paragraphs and essays is a primary goal of any middle school Language Arts writing curriculum. Even though students have been instructed in the writing process since third grade, many of them graduate from the eighth grade with no concrete idea of what it means to write well-structured and well-supported essays. *Expanding the Writing Process with Elaboration* shows the process of expanding and developing ideas. Although the techniques are not new, the approach is novel. The "elaboration process" takes students beyond writing well-structured paragraphs, referred to as Level One, to writing essays in Level Two. Level Two is a process-oriented approach, formatted in sequential order and reinforced by practice exercises. These exercises are not meant to be random or routine strategies, as past attempts to teach these skills have been. The two levels combined equip students with the necessary skills for expanding and elaborating their ideas, while providing a structure for their papers and a list of techniques they can rely upon for future essays.

Instead of inserting these techniques into convenient spaces in lesson plans, teachers should proceed from the beginning of the book and move forward in a methodical manner. The separation and emphasis of elaboration techniques allows teachers the opportunity for meaningful instruction of the essay writing process found in Level Two, which will propel students' writing to new levels of creativity far beyond the average compositions witnessed today.

After implementing the strategies contained in this workbook, students will own the techniques necessary to expand and develop their ideas. Their writing performance will improve, and their scores on state writing assessment tests will soar. They will be on their way to reaching their full potential as writers by *Expanding the Writing Process with Elaboration*.

How to Use This Book

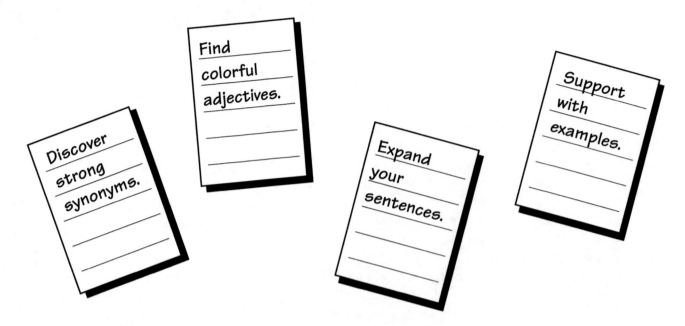

The materials in this workbook should be used as an integral part of the writing curriculum. Each item in the table of contents is a lesson plan in itself, and grammar instruction can be easily integrated into many of the exercises in both sections. Part One focuses on the introduction and application of elaboration techniques involved in paragraph writing. A section titled "Tips for Writing Effective Sentences" provides ample instruction on sentence improvement.

Part Two focuses on the development of the essay through the application of these same techniques. Sample essays are included in order to model effective elaboration.

The Teaching Guide prefacing each part of this book explains objectives and instructions on the various elaboration techniques. Answer keys have been provided at the end of the book for exercises that require specific answers.

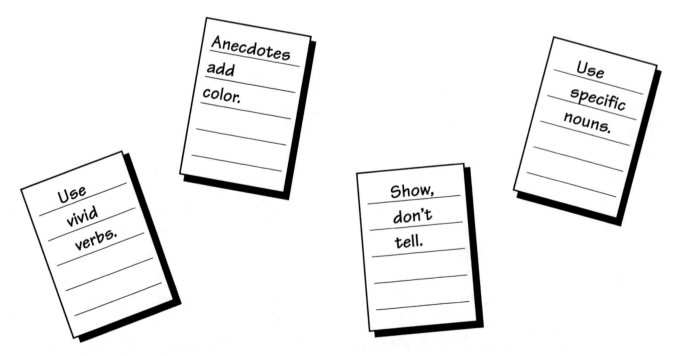

Teaching Guide for Part One— Writing Elaborated Paragraphs

Objectives

- To use strong, colorful action verbs instead of overused, dull verbs to make writing more detailed and interesting
- To use original and vivid adjectives instead of common, boring adjectives to make writing more exciting and colorful
- To expand sentences by building upon them
- To use examples that provide support and information
- To use an anecdote to explain or prove an idea
- To use details that create pictures by appealing to the senses
- To use direct quotes and/or dialogue to explain or prove a point
- To use similes that further explain comparisons
- To use facts and statistics to make writing more convincing
- To read peer writing models in order to identify when elaboration techniques are used and when they are not used
- To score peer writing models in order to understand the specific criteria by which student writing will be assessed

Instructions for Part One—Elaborating the Paragraph

1. Enlarge, post, and introduce page 7, "Characteristics of Elaborated Paragraphs," and define "elaboration."

2. Practice with strong verbs, vivid adjectives, exact nouns, expanding sentences and "Show! Don't tell!" sentences, pages 8–27.

3. Introduce "Elaborate with Examples," pages 28–32. Remind students to use strong verbs, vivid adjectives, and exact nouns.

4. Introduce "Elaborate with Anecdotes," pages 33–38. Focus on anecdotes which contain a beginning, middle, and end; emphasize that in order for anecdotes to be effective, they must be related to and support the main idea of a paragraph.

5. Combine the use of examples and anecdotes to support the main idea.

6. Introduce "Elaborating with Sensory Images," pages 39–43.

Teaching Guide for Part One— Writing Elaborated Paragraphs *(cont.)*

Instructions for Part One *(cont.)*

7. Combine the use of examples, anecdotes, and sensory words, page 44. Use passages from your literature or grammar books to further illustrate these techniques.

8. Introduce "Elaborate with Quotes and Dialogue," page 45.

9. Combine the use of quotes, dialogue, examples, and an anecdote, pages 46-47. At this time, instruct students to insert vivid adjectives and substitute strong verbs and exact nouns during the editing stage. Include "Elaborate with Similes," pages 48–49.

10. Introduce "Elaborate with Facts and Statistics," pages 50–51. Use passages from your literature or grammar books to further illustrate these techniques.

11. Read and discuss "Tips for Writing Effective Sentences," pages 52–53. This is an excellent time to review the parts of speech and punctuation.

12. Introduce and explain the "Scoring Key," page 54. You may need to simplify the key for lower-level students.

13. Read "Models of Elaborated Paragraphs" that have been scored, pages 55–57.

14. Score models of elaborated paragraphs with students, pages 58–60.

15. Review remaining points on "Characteristics of Elaborated Paragraphs" poster, on page 7. This is also a good time to review sentence structure and mechanics.

Characteristics of Elaborated Paragraphs

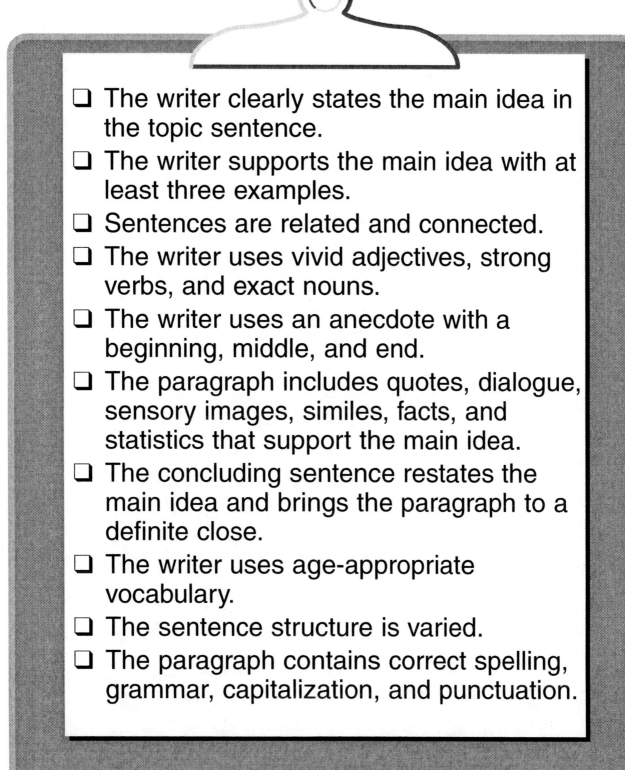

❑ The writer clearly states the main idea in the topic sentence.

❑ The writer supports the main idea with at least three examples.

❑ Sentences are related and connected.

❑ The writer uses vivid adjectives, strong verbs, and exact nouns.

❑ The writer uses an anecdote with a beginning, middle, and end.

❑ The paragraph includes quotes, dialogue, sensory images, similes, facts, and statistics that support the main idea.

❑ The concluding sentence restates the main idea and brings the paragraph to a definite close.

❑ The writer uses age-appropriate vocabulary.

❑ The sentence structure is varied.

❑ The paragraph contains correct spelling, grammar, capitalization, and punctuation.

Elaborate with Strong Verbs

Strong and precise verbs help to paint a vivid picture in the reader's mind.

Directions: Examine the following pairs of sentences. Note that the second sentence in each pair contains a stronger and more precise verb. The sentences with the stronger verbs should serve as models for future writing.

1a. I want a chocolate candy bar.

b. I crave a chocolate candy bar.

2a. The children said, "We saw a spider on the wall."

b. The children screamed, "We saw a spider on the wall!"

3a. Jane got the book from me.

b. Jane grabbed the book from me.

4a. Jack went to the neighbors for help.

b. Jack raced to the neighbors for help.

5a. The policeman saw blood on the suspect's hand.

b. The policeman detected blood on the suspect's hand.

6a. The Red Cross got every person who volunteered to collect toys.

b. The Red Cross inspired every person who volunteered to collect toys.

7a. The nurse went to the ailing patient.

b. The nurse hurried to the ailing patient.

8a. The architect made the plans for the new hospital.

b. The architect designed the plans for the new hospital.

9a. The dog found the bone he had buried.

b. The dog uncovered the bone he had buried.

10a. The girl went down the hill on her snowboard.

b. The girl sped down the hill on her snowboard.

Replace Dull Verbs with Precise Verbs

Directions: Replace the common, overused verbs on the left with three stronger, more precise verbs from the list below. The first one has been done for you.

1. **turn**	spin	twist	twirl
2. **see**	_____	_____	_____
3. **run**	_____	_____	_____
4. **walk**	_____	_____	_____
5. **wander**	_____	_____	_____
6. **say**	_____	_____	_____
7. **eat**	_____	_____	_____
8. **make**	_____	_____	_____
9. **give**	_____	_____	_____
10. **go**	_____	_____	_____
11. **find**	_____	_____	_____
12. **want**	_____	_____	_____

locate	limp	devour	discover
leave	present	twirl	stare
desire	glimpse	crave	meander
offer	roam	design	hurry
crawl	create	wish	consume
race	twist	drift	strut
declare	detect	dash	construct
spin	reply	respond	furnish
gorge	withdraw	observe	depart

Discover Strong Synonyms for Weak Verbs

Directions: Replace the common, overused verbs on the left with three stronger, more vivid verbs from the list below.

1. **cut** _____ _____ _____

2. **drink** _____ _____ _____

3. **take** _____ _____ _____

4. **put** _____ _____ _____

5. **get** _____ _____ _____

6. **ask** _____ _____ _____

7. **laugh** _____ _____ _____

8. **think** _____ _____ _____

9. **use** _____ _____ _____

10. **save** _____ _____ _____

operate	tear	cackle	question
pull	arrange	employ	imagine
contemplate	grab	inquire	sip
store	obtain	possess	giggle
gulp	utilize	snatch	conserve
place	believe	preserve	swallow
clip	quiz	snip	chuckle
hand	acquire		

Replace Overused Verbs with Exciting Verbs

Directions: Cross out the underlined dull, overused verb in the sentence. Write a stronger, more precise verb above it. Use words from your lists from the previous pages to help you. The first one has been done for you.

1. He ~~ran~~ raced toward the finish line.

2. I think about owning my own boat some day.

3. The librarian put the books on the shelf in alphabetical order.

4. The student found the Caribbean Islands on the map.

5. The sixth graders made forts out of toothpicks and craft sticks.

6. She said, "I don't want any more broccoli."

7. The family saved canned goods and bottled water for the snowstorm.

8. The hairdresser cut the dry ends off my hair.

9. The Smiths got two acres on the west side of a sunny mountain.

10. Dad went under the house to look for our lost kitten.

11. She has two trophies from skateboarding competitions.

12. The boys saw the stand-up comedian.

13. The judge thought about his important decision.

14. The unhappy baby took the bottle of milk from her mother.

15. The plane will leave at approximately 1:00 P.M.

Vivid Verb Picture Scavenger Hunt

1. Cut out each vivid verb, below.

2. Cut out a picture from a magazine or newspaper that represents each vivid verb.

3. Glue pictures on a piece of construction paper. Above each picture, glue the appropriate vivid verb. Write the definition of the verb below the picture.

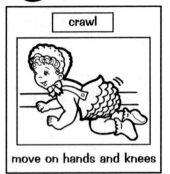

crawl

move on hands and knees

construct	operate	contemplate
observe	cackle	employ
snatch	crawl	twist
devour	meander	race
furnish	rescue	battle

Elaborate with Descriptive Adjectives

You can create a lasting picture in the reader's mind by using vivid, descriptive adjectives in your writing.

Directions: Examine the following pairs of sentences. Note that the second sentence in each pair contains more descriptive adjectives. The sentences with the descriptive adjectives should serve as models for future writing.

1a. The car sped past us.

  b. The sleek black car sped past us.

2a. The Castros live on the street around the corner.

  b. The Castros live on the tree-lined street around the corner.

3a. The boat sailed across the ocean.

  b. The boat sailed across the rough black ocean.

4a. The class decorated the room with streamers.

  b. The class decorated the dreary room with colorful streamers.

5a. Mr. Hellman speaks with an accent.

  b. Mr. Hellman speaks with a heavy German accent.

6a. This radio can fit into your pocket.

  b. This tiny radio can fit into your coat pocket.

7a. We saw some fish at the Florida Aquarium.

  b. We saw some unusual tropical fish at the Florida Aquarium.

8a. The snow covered the streets.

  b. The slushy, melting snow covered the streets.

9a. The cook added the tomatoes to the salad.

  b. The cook added two ripe tomatoes to the spinach salad.

10a. The gorilla was the star of the movie.

  b. The enormous, hairy gorilla was the star of the movie.

Replace Dull Adjectives
with Vivid Adjectives

Directions: Replace the underlined, overused adjective with a more vivid adjective from the list below. Write the adjective on the blank.

1. a <u>good</u> friend _____
2. <u>little</u> toys _____
3. a <u>nice</u> person _____
4. a <u>bad</u> boy _____
5. a <u>big</u> book _____
6. a <u>well-known</u> model _____
7. a <u>high</u> hill _____
8. an <u>ugly</u> car _____
9. a <u>funny</u> joke _____
10. <u>great</u> news _____
11. a <u>good</u> student _____
12. a <u>cool</u> story _____
13. a <u>great</u> gift _____
14. <u>pretty</u> features _____
15. a <u>bad</u> crime _____
16. a <u>big</u> roach _____
17. a <u>good</u> sister _____
18. a <u>bad</u> accident _____
19. a <u>good</u> dancer _____
20. a <u>high</u> building _____

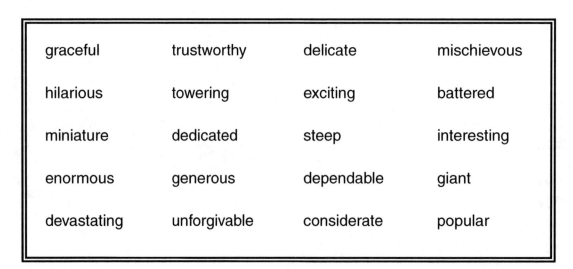

graceful	trustworthy	delicate	mischievous
hilarious	towering	exciting	battered
miniature	dedicated	steep	interesting
enormous	generous	dependable	giant
devastating	unforgivable	considerate	popular

Elaborate with Colorful Adjectives

Directions: Fill in the blanks with the descriptive, vivid adjectives from the list below.

1. The _____ motor bikers raced around the _____ track.

2. As we looked down the _____ path, we heard a _____ noise.

3. Our _____ family looks forward to our _____ reunions.

4. The burglar sped through the _____ streets and into the _____ alley.

5. We patiently sat in the _____ bleachers, but we were uncomfortable.

6. The _____ divers rescued the _____ woman from the sea.

7. The _____ student body sat in _____ silence during the assembly.

8. That _____ house has a _____ foundation.

9. The _____ scarf was given to me by my grandmother.

10. My _____ sister made me clean my _____ room.

11. The woman's _____ hair reached down to her knees.

12. The _____ truck screeched around the corner with _____ speed.

annual	noisy	shadowy	experienced
dark	flowered	well-built	well-lit
older	crowded	excited	anxious
fire	messy	loud	narrow
frightened	closely-knit	muddy	high
solid	long		

Spot the Vivid Adjectives

Directions: Read the following paragraph. Find, underline, and list 25 vivid adjectives that help to paint a colorful picture in the reader's mind.

Fun-loving people from all over our wonderful county should attend the Hillsborough County Fair this month. The fair is sure to guarantee excitement for the family. For the sweet-toothed toddlers and teens, delicious pink cotton candy and yummy chocolate fudge await them in the concession stands. No one will be able to resist the cheesy pizza, greasy French fries, and tasty corn dogs for lunch or dinner. Thrilling and exhilarating rides promise daring teens and adventurous adults an exciting and wild time. Challenging midway games and the video arcade always attract winners as well. Adults of all ages will enjoy cultural exhibits, a magnificent horse show, and many talented singers and graceful dancers. Be sure not to miss the entertaining event which takes place every year in February at the County Fairgrounds.

1. _____

2. _____

3. _____

4. _____

5. _____

6. _____

7. _____

8. _____

9. _____

10. _____

11. _____

12. _____

13. _____

14. _____

15. _____

16. _____

17. _____

18. _____

19. _____

20. _____

21. _____

22. _____

23. _____

24. _____

25. _____

Spot the Vivid Adjectives *(cont.)*

Directions: Read the following paragraph. Find, underline, and list 24 vivid adjectives on the lines provided.

American teens today face serious peer pressures. They are put into uncomfortable situations in and out of school. At school, influential or popular kids may tempt them to skip classes, be disrespectful, or violate safety procedures. At parties, the most tempting challenges may be to smoke or inhale dangerous substances, drink potent alcoholic beverages, or participate in illegal activities like stealing or joyriding. At home, there are insurmountable expectations from parents, like achieving awesome grades, having perfect attendance, and being involved in extracurricular activities such as sports or art classes. The effects of these continuous pressures may cause mental stress, physical discomforts, like headaches and stomach pains, and even emotional and social problems leading to depression. Teens in America are growing up too fast and with too much pressure.

1. _____

2. _____

3. _____

4. _____

5. _____

6. _____

7. _____

8. _____

9. _____

10. _____

11. _____

12. _____

13. _____

14. _____

15. _____

16. _____

17. _____

18. _____

19. _____

20. _____

21. _____

22. _____

23. _____

24. _____

Vivid Adjective Picture Scavenger Hunt

1. Cut out each vivid adjective, below.

2. Cut out a picture from a magazine or newspaper that represents each vivid adjective.

3. Glue pictures on a piece of construction paper. Above each picture, glue the appropriate vivid adjective. Write the definition of the adjective below the picture.

comic

humorous makes me laugh

eccentric	angry	elderly
patriotic	athletic	frustrated
vivacious	enthusiatic	frightened
suspicious	comical	juvenile
sparkling	sorrowful	embarassed

Elaborate with Exact Nouns

Exact nouns help to create a precise image in the reader's mind. You provide more accurate information on a subject when your nouns are specific.

Directions: Examine the following pairs of sentences. Note that the second sentence in each pair contains a more specific noun. The sentences with the more specific nouns should serve as models for future writing.

1a. The man walking in our neighborhood scares me.

  b. The stranger walking in our neighborhood scares me.

2a. She worked as a nurse during the war.

  b. She worked as a nurse during the American Revolution.

3a. Ray Bradbury's stories are full of good things.

  b. Ray Bradbury's mysteries are full of suspense and excitement.

4a. We read about something that exploded above some state.

  b. We read about a spacecraft that exploded above Florida.

5a. Please get that insect off me!

  b. Please get that mosquito off me!

6a. If the people forget their lines, the play will be bad.

  b. If the actors forget their lines, the play will be bad.

7a. Some things provide daily calcium for the body.

  b. Milk and cheese provide daily calcium for the body.

8a. All of the persons performed well in the races.

  b. All of the contestants performed well in the relays.

9a. The two people ran the track in not much time.

  b. The two female athletes ran the track in less than two minutes.

10a. Mr. Morgan will perform his act for the next show.

  b. Mr. Morgan will perform his magic for the next hospital fundraiser.

Exciting Exact Nouns Versus Common Nouns

Directions: Write the common noun from the list below that describes the more specific pair of nouns in the first two columns.

Specific Noun	Specific Noun	Common Noun
chocolate	vanilla	
carnival	parade	
squash	broccoli	
doctor	nurse	
ocean	space	
shuttle	rocket	
recliner	rocker	
yacht	submarine	
hockey	tennis	
kidney	lung	
cobra	python	
roller coaster	ferris wheel	
toaster	blender	
rifle	pistol	
pitbull	beagle	
Protestant	Catholic	
minister	priest	
wallpaper	curtains	
reading	stamp collecting	
encyclopedia	newspaper	

decorations	locations	dogs	spacecraft
guns	vegetables	careers	organs
snakes	sports	boats	appliances
chairs	events	religions	clergy
references	rides	ice cream	hobbies

Replace Common Nouns
with Exact Nouns

Directions: Replace the underlined noun with a more exact noun. Write it on the blank.

1. A man dropped his <u>project</u> on the living room floor. _____

2. Someday I am going to own that <u>car</u>. _____

3. The <u>men</u> buried a large chest with gold coins under the bridge.
   _____

4. The <u>lady</u> arranged the books on the shelf very carefully. _____

5. The <u>man</u> ran across the finish line and won first prize. _____

6. We ate a lot of <u>snacks</u> at the movies. _____

7. Our <u>club</u> raised $300.00 to help underprivileged children in Asia. _____

8. The <u>creature</u> made funny noises as he swung from branch to branch. _____

9. The polar bear waded into the ocean and caught a <u>fish</u> for dinner. _____

10. That <u>place</u> was filled to capacity on Valentine's Day. _____

11. I was so happy to win that <u>prize</u>. _____

12. The <u>guy</u> at the store gave me lotion for my insect bites. _____

13. We should be fearful of poisonous <u>snakes</u>. _____

14. Mozart was a very talented <u>person</u>. _____

15. We decorated the living room with a lot of <u>flowers</u>.
    _____

16. That <u>reptile</u> devoured the mouse before our very eyes. _____

17. Eating various <u>citrus products</u> will help you to avoid colds. _____

18. The <u>picture</u> covering the north wall depicts a beautiful country landscape.
    _____

19. The <u>gentleman</u> in the striped shirt blew his whistle when the basketball player fouled.
    _____

20. The <u>player</u> threw a 50-yard pass to the running back. _____

Elaborate with Expanded Sentences

By answering the questions, who, what, what kind, where, when, why, and how, you can elaborate on simple sentences.

Directions: Expand the sentences below by adding answers for the questions in parentheses. Rewrite the complete sentence. The first one has been done for you.

1. The (what kind?) singer signed autographs (when?).

    The rap singer signed autographs after the concert.

2. I failed the (what?) test (why?).

3. (when?) the little boy was crying (why?).

4. We saw the (what kind?) airplane (where?).

5. The (what kind?) man paced (how?) as he waited for the announcement.

6. The (what kind?) hurricane (how?) damaged (what?).

7. The (what kind?) batter hit the (what kind?) ball (how?) (where?).

8. Snakes move (how?) (where?).

9. The principal from (where?) announced the (what kind?) winners.

10. (when?) I broke my leg (how?).

11. The tornado struck (where?) and damaged several (what kind?) buildings.

Answering Questions to Elaborate Sentences

Directions: Elaborate the simple sentences below by answering at least two of the following questions: who, what, what kind, where, when, why, and how. Rewrite the complete sentence. The first one has been done for you.

1. The students studied history.
   The 8th grade students at Hill Middle School studied United States History last summer.

2. They went to the theater. _____

3. The child was hit. _____

4. The zoo is fun. _____

5. The student was mad. _____

6. The man made dinner. _____

7. The boy likes animals. _____

8. The woman gave the orders. _____

9. The kids crossed the street. _____

10. The students were issued lockers. _____

11. The contestants swam in the competition. _____

12. The cards were arranged in order. _____

13. Chad broke one of the glasses. _____

14. The bookstore specializes in novels. _____

15. Each of the states has a climate. _____

Answering Questions
to Elaborate Sentences *(cont.)*

16. The guide lists the movies to be shown.

    _____

    _____

17. Look for the elements on the label.

    _____

    _____

18. Ornaments of all shapes decorate our tree.

    _____

    _____

19. The supervisor had a meeting.

    _____

    _____

20. The woman forgot her appointment.

    _____

    _____

21. Constructing models is fun.

    _____

    _____

22. The man sitting on the beach became sunburned.

    _____

    _____

23. The earthquake damaged the building.

    _____

    _____

24. The dogs are for sale in that store.

    _____

    _____

Elaborate by Showing, Not Telling

Create a picture in the reader's mind by writing sentences that show what happened rather than telling what happened. You can do this by replacing linking verbs with active verbs, and of course, by using more vivid adjectives.

Directions: Examine the following sentence pairs. Note that the second sentence in each pair shows the feeling or event instead of telling it. The second sentences should serve as models for future writing.

1a. The little girl looked in the window.
 b. The little girl pressed so close to the window that her breath fogged the glass.

2a. My mother and I walked and looked at the glass window of the chapel.
 b. My mother and I would take walks to watch the glow of the chapel's stained glass.

3a. The sorority sisters decorated the halls.
 b. The sorority sisters cheerfully decorated the halls with green garlands and streamers of red crepe paper.

4a. I climbed the fence.
 b. I climbed up the wooden fence and got a splinter in the palm of my hand.

5a. Dominique gives candy to her customers.
 b. Dominique graciously presents sweet treats of sugar-dusted wafers and creamy milk chocolate to her customers.

6a. The table was decorated for Christmas.
 b. Bright-red ribbons, dimly-lit candles, and a green cloth decorated the Christmas table.

7a. The lights sent signals from village to village.
 b. Twinkling like cheerful flares, the lights sent signals from village to village.

8a. She felt embarrassed when she fell.
 b. She tripped and fell backward, then stood up with blushing cheeks and shaking hands.

9a. I get nervous when I give a speech.
 b. Whenever I am scheduled to give a speech, I suffer with wet, clammy hands and butterflies in my stomach.

10a. Two people are playing hockey.
 b. Two hockey players take unsuccessful swipes at the puck.

Show! Don't Tell!

Directions: Examine the following passages. Note that the second story "shows" rather "tells." Passage B should serve as your model for writing your own "showing" passages below and on the next page.

Passage A

My mornings are crazy. I am rushing all the time. Sometimes I miss my bus and arrive late to school.

Passage B

I awaken to the annoying buzz of my alarm clock at 6:30 a.m. I am anything but ready to face the day ahead of me. I drag myself to the bathroom, where I brush my teeth, take a quick shower, and wash and dry my hair. After changing outfits three or four times, I run down the stairs, let my dog out, and inhale my breakfast. I scramble for my books and jacket, then race out the front door. I barely make it to my bus on time. Once in the seat, I heave a sigh of relief because I will not be late to school today.

Directions: Write a passage that "shows" rather than "tells" for each of the sentences below and on the next page.

The mall is crowded in December.

_____

_____

_____

_____

_____

_____

_____

Show! Don't Tell! *(cont.)*

I live on a very busy street.

_____

_____

_____

_____

_____

_____

_____

My birthday party is going to be the best ever.

_____

_____

_____

_____

_____

_____

_____

I have a fun hobby.

_____

_____

_____

_____

_____

_____

_____

Elaborate with Examples

Using examples will help you elaborate your writing and make it more interesting to the reader. Examples can effectively support your main idea. They are especially useful in defending an opinion.

Directions: Read the descriptions below. The topic sentence (which states the main idea) is written in italics. Find the examples that support the topic sentence and underline them. The first one has been done for you.

Coach Azul knows what it takes to keep his team physically fit. Three mornings a week, they <u>work out in the weight room for 30 minutes, jog two miles around the school track, and end with 25 sit-ups.</u>

1. *Without an education, you won't be able to afford the things you want.* You won't earn enough money to purchase your dream car, wear stylish clothes, or live in a comfortable and luxurious home.

2. *Statistics show that vegetarians seem to be healthier than meat-eaters.* They have much lower rates of cancer and heart disease, they maintain weight within a healthy range, and their blood pressure and cholesterol counts are much better than average.

3. *Studies show that smoking is bad for your health.* Thousands of smokers die each year from lung cancer and other diseases. Other harmful effects of smoking include developing a smoker's cough and running out of breath during strenuous physical activities.

4. *My grandpa is a generous person.* He feeds and shelters stray animals, cooks for the homeless, and contributes to charities. He always seems to be giving to someone or something.

5. *Our school cafeteria food needs plenty of improvement.* Often the milk is sour and the bread is stale. But worst of all, bugs are sometimes found in the cereal.

Elaborate with Examples *(cont.)*

6. *Going camping provides fun for the whole family.* Bird-lovers can sit at the campsite with their binoculars all day. Hikers can take off with a backpack and a bagged lunch. Later, everyone can sit around the campfire and toast marshmallows.

7. *Living in a northern state offers many opportunities for recreation.* Snow skiing, snowboarding, and ice skating are favorite sports. Many people also like to snowshoe and go sledding.

8. *Hot spices and ingredients make up a large part of most Mexican recipes.* Cayenne, red pepper, and chili powder are found in most foods. Many Mexican pantries include jalapeño peppers and green chiles.

9. *Mom takes good care of me when I'm sick.* She prepares her delicious chicken soup when I have a cold, and she makes sure that I have a comfortable bed with plenty of warm coverings. She even spends time playing card games with me.

10. *A healthy diet includes foods that are low in calories.* Celery and carrot sticks, lettuce with fat-free salad dressing, and a variety of fruits and green vegetables provide essential vitamins as well as energy for sports and other activities.

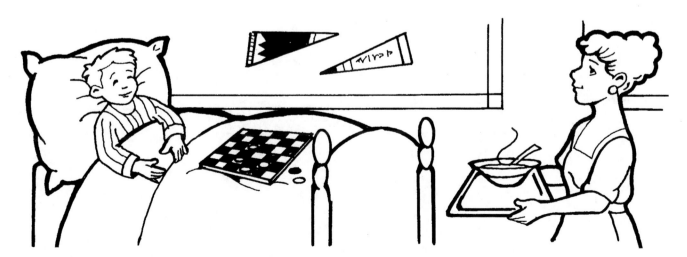

Support Your Topic Sentence with Examples

Directions: Write three examples supporting the underlined topic sentences listed below. The first one has been done for you.

<u>Tourists should visit Florida.</u>

    1. <u>It offers many sandy and beautiful beaches.</u>

    2. <u>It has many amusement parks.</u>

    3. <u>It has several thrilling and exciting water-theme parks.</u>

<u>Most American teens experience peer pressure.</u>

    1. _____

    2. _____

    3. _____

<u>Amusement parks provide fun for the entire family.</u>

    1. _____

    2. _____

    3. _____

<u>My best friend is a very trustworthy person.</u>

    1. _____

    2. _____

    3. _____

<u>Successful students possess exceptional qualities.</u>

    1. _____

    2. _____

    3. _____

<u>American citizens enjoy many freedoms.</u>

    1. _____

    2. _____

    3. _____

Write an Elaborated Paragraph

Directions: Write an elaborated paragraph on one of the five topic sentences on page 30. Refer to the guidelines at the bottom of this page. Remember to elaborate with vivid adjectives, strong verbs, and specific nouns. Study the example below.

> **Example:**
>
> Tourists from all over the world should visit Florida.
>
> The Sunshine State, as Florida is called, offers many beautiful and sandy beaches. It also has several amusement parks with exciting rides and games for the whole family. If you like water-theme parks, you should know that Florida is the home to "Adventure Island" in Tampa and "Typhoon Lagoon" in Disneyworld. You're sure to have a memorable vacation if you visit this state.

• Clearly state the main idea of your paragraph in the topic sentence.
• Support your main idea with at least three examples.
• Use vivid adjectives, strong verbs, and exact nouns.
• End your paragraph with a concluding sentence that restates the main idea.

Write an Elaborated Paragraph *(cont.)*

Directions: Write an elaborated paragraph for each of the following topic sentences. Refer to the guidelines on page 31 for help.

1. I am a very responsible student.

_____

_____

_____

_____

_____

_____

_____

_____

2. School cafeterias should have rules.

_____

_____

_____

_____

_____

_____

_____

_____

3. I have an excellent teacher.

_____

_____

_____

_____

_____

_____

_____

_____

Elaborate with Anecdotes

An anecdote is a short account of an interesting or amusing incident. It is often a personal experience. The anecdote supports the main point of a paragraph by briefly describing an event. It should include a beginning, middle, and end.

Directions: Read the elaborated paragraphs below. The anecdotes have been underlined for you. Note how they support the main idea of the paragraphs, which are underlined in with broken lines.

When I was in kindergarten, my teacher told my mother that I had leadership qualities. Looking back, I see that people followed my lead then as they do now. They asked my opinion on things and often applauded my decisions. In elementary school, my classmates elected me as their class president, safety patrol captain, and student council representative. One time in fourth grade, one of our classmates had tripped and fallen on the playground during recess. Almost everyone started laughing and making fun of her. I admit that it was a little funny, but instead of following the crowd, I helped her up and shared my snack with her. When the other kids saw me doing this, they stopped laughing and went back to playing. Some of them even came up and offered their help. Sarah told me the next day how much better I had made her feel. As you can see, people follow my leadership no matter what the situation.

I am part of the student body who believes that students don't have enough passing time between classes. Whether you need to visit your locker, go to the restroom, or dash across campus to the gym, it's hard to beat the clock. Trying to do any one of the things mentioned above, not to mention socializing a little with your friends, is sure to guarantee an unexcused tardy. About a month ago on my way to science class, I realized that I had forgotten my research report in my locker. I hustled back to the second wing where my locker is located and tried to open it. Unfortunately, it was jammed. Unsuccessful at opening it, I raced back to make my class on time. I wasn't in my seat when the tardy bell rang and received an unexcused tardy. I was late, and I was penalized for not having my report that day. What happened to me happens to many people. I believe that adding a few extra minutes to our passing time would help us all to be better students.

Spot the Supportive Anecdote

Directions: Paragraphs A and B each contain anecdotes. Find them and underline them. However, only one anecdote strongly supports the main idea. Identify which paragraph contains the strongly supportive anecdote by writing a check mark on the blank line following the paragraph.

Paragraph A

Most of my friends have traits that I truly admire, but my friend Richie is the most helpful person I have ever known. He does favors for classmates, such as loaning them school supplies or helping them with their homework. Being the oldest brother in a family of four, he is always ready to help his mom with his younger siblings or the household chores. I will never forget the time I broke my leg at the roller-skating rink. Richie was the first one there to offer his help. Being much taller and bigger than I am, he carried me on his back to a comfortable chair and then called my parents. He sat and talked with me the entire time while our other friends continued to skate and have fun. Not only is Richie helpful, but he's the best friend anyone could have. _____

Paragraph B

I consider my friend Sylvia to be a very humorous person. When I am feeling low or I'm in a bad mood, there's Sylvia to cheer me up with funny jokes and facial expressions. Just watching her and the crazy things she does really lifts my spirits. At lunch last week, I was very angry about something that happened during my third period math class. She came up and offered me half her sandwich. Then she offered to explain the math homework to me. Sylvia and I have been friends since elementary school because of her humor. Teachers always refer to her as the class comedian. Her mom says she always makes her laugh, too. If I didn't have a comical friend like Sylvia, I think I would have a very boring time at school. Who knows? Maybe someday we'll all see her on *Saturday Night Live*.

_____

Analyze an Elaborated Paragraph

Directions: Read the elaborated paragraph and then answer the questions below.

I believe that I am responsible for my age. When I compare myself to other eighth graders, I realize that I have a lot more chores to perform. Perhaps this is because my mother died when I was nine years old. After my mother died, my father gave me many more responsibilities than the average nine-year-old. For example, it is my job to make sure everyone in the family has clean clothes to wear every day. One time I forgot to do my own laundry, and my Dad wanted to teach me a lesson I wouldn't forget. He made me wear clothes out of my dirty clothes hamper. All day long at school, I kept hoping that no one would notice that my shirt was wrinkled and my socks were dirty. Boy, was I humiliated! I made sure that never happened again. In addition to doing the laundry, I take care of my little sister after school and prepare dinner for all of us. On Saturday mornings, I have a babysitting job. I work at my Dad's office in the afternoon. All of these responsibilities make me feel grown up and responsible, even though I'm only thirteen and small for my age.

1. Write the sentence that shows the main idea of this paragraph.

   _____

   _____

2. What personal trait is the writer elaborating about?

   _____

3. List five examples that support the fact that this writer thinks that he/she is responsible.

   _____

   _____

   _____

4. What are the beginning, middle, and end of the anecdote?

   _____

   _____

5. Which vivid adjective lets the reader know how the writer felt when he/she forgot to do the laundry? What does it mean? _____

   _____

6. Write the closing sentence. _____

   _____

   _____

Elaborate with Examples
and an Anecdote

Directions: You have read an elaborated paragraph about a person and his/her positive individual trait. Now it is your turn to write about one of your positive individual traits. For help in choosing a trait, refer to the list on the following page. Select a trait and write an elaborated paragraph on the space provided below. Refer to the guidelines at the bottom of this page for help.

_____

_____

_____

_____

_____

_____

_____

_____

_____

_____

_____

- Clearly state the main idea of your paragraph in the topic sentence.
- Support your main idea with at least three examples.
- Include a strongly supportive anecdote that has a beginning, middle, and end.
- End your paragraph with a concluding sentence that restates the main idea.

Elaborate with Examples
and an Anecdote (cont.)

Positive Individual Traits	
trustworthy	outgoing
patient	athletic
mature	creative
honest	generous
responsible	dependable
understanding	kind
intelligent	non-judgmental
considerate	humorous
helpful	forgiving
determined	artistic
thoughtful	appreciative
loyal	cooperative
talented	adventurous

Elaborate with Examples
and an Anecdote *(cont.)*

Directions: Now, think about a positive trait you admire in someone else. You may refer back to the previous page for ideas. Write an elaborated paragraph on the space below. Refer to the guidelines at the bottom of this page.

_____

_____

_____

_____

_____

_____

_____

_____

_____

_____

- Clearly state the main idea of your paragraph in the topic sentence.
- Support your main idea with at least three examples.
- Include a strongly supportive anecdote that has a beginning, middle, and end.
- End your paragraph with a concluding sentence that restates the main idea.

Elaborate with Sensory Images

As writers, we can create vivid pictures by using words that appeal to our readers' senses. Words that engage the senses of hearing, sight, touch, taste, and smell will help readers to experience what you're describing.

Directions: Read the sentences below and then write the sensory words on the provided lines. The first one has been done for you.

1. The old and rusty steel door creaked as we opened it.

   old, rusty, creaked

2. I remember warm, sunny afternoons at Grandmother's lake when we swam and splashed water at each other.

3. The taste of sweet and sticky cotton candy always reminds me of the exciting carnival days I enjoyed as a child.

4. I could smell the aroma of corn dogs and greasy French fries from six blocks away.

5. My hands felt clammy and my heart beat faster and faster as the roller coaster began its journey.

6. The sour pickles, sweet funnel cakes, and salty corn on the cob were my favorite foods.

7. The old tomcat was easily identified by his torn ears, scruffy coat, and missing front tooth.

8. The winner beat his hands upon his chest and stomped his feet on the pavement stones.

9. It was a cold, bleak, and gloomy winter day in January.

10. Observers below sensed the fright on the climber's face as he grasped, clutched, and hugged the mountainside.

Spot the Sensory Images

Directions: Read the paragraph below. Notice where the writer appeals to the various senses. Above each underlined sensory word or phrase, write which of the five senses it engages: **sight**, **sound**, **taste**, **smell**, or **touch**.

After a boring day at school, I <u>stomped</u> up the <u>slippery</u> steps and into the <u>narrow</u> aisle of our school bus. A wave of <u>blistering</u> heat descended upon me as I <u>collapsed</u> into a vacant seat. It had rained all day; the air in the bus smelled <u>stale</u> and the temperature was very <u>humid</u>. The <u>black leather</u> seats felt <u>sticky</u>, making for an uncomfortable ride home. As usual, kids <u>shouted</u>, <u>yelled</u>, and <u>laughed</u> in the <u>crowded</u> bus. I caught the whiff of someone's <u>grape-flavored</u> bubble gum. My stomach <u>growled</u> with hunger. I could practically taste my dad's delicious home-baked <u>chocolate-chip brownies</u>. I wished to arrive home as soon as possible. As the driver approached my street, he <u>pressed</u> down on the <u>squeaky</u> brakes, and then my stop was in sight. I rose and <u>dashed</u> out of the bus only to realize I had left my bookbag behind.

My friends and I sat on the <u>hard</u> <u>wooden</u> bleachers and watched the exciting baseball game. "Strike one!" <u>yelled</u> the umpire, and the crowd <u>cheered</u>. I ate handfuls of <u>salty</u> <u>peanuts</u> and washed them down with a <u>thick</u>, <u>sweet</u> <u>chocolate</u> malt. The air smelled of <u>buttery</u> <u>popcorn</u> and <u>greasy</u> <u>pizza</u> from the vendors walking up and down the aisles. The umpire <u>hollered</u> "Strike two!" and my friend and I gave each other a <u>high-five</u>. I <u>shivered</u> as the <u>sun</u> slipped behind a cloud. "Strike three!" came the <u>call</u>. The crowd <u>screamed</u> and <u>cheered</u>.

List the Sensory Images

Directions: Read the description below. Notice how the writer appeals to the various senses. Find, underline, and list 30 sensory words or phrases that help you to experience what the writer is describing.

I will always remember my visit to the most fascinating rainforest in South America. The air was moist and smelled of moss and rich dirt. I observed white, fluffy clouds gracefully floating above the branches of the towering trees. Standing thickly, the trees provided a canopy that allowed only thin streams of light to push through. Plants of various sizes and shapes, some pointed, some round, blended in with the natural setting of greens, browns, and yellows. Underfoot, the ground was soft, mushy, and slippery. I heard the sounds of rippling water and the gentle rustling of leaves in the near distance. As I made my way through each curving path, I smelled sweet, fresh flowers. I have to admit that at times, my hands felt clammy and my heart thumped a little faster whenever unfamiliar, croaking creatures wearing coats of red, yellow, and neon green, hopped across my path. They must have been as timid as the stranger walking through their home. In retrospect, my adventure in the rainforest was captivating and full of surprises.

1._____   11._____   21._____

2._____   12._____   22._____

3._____   13._____   23._____

4._____   14._____   24._____

5._____   15._____   25._____

6._____   16._____   26._____

7._____   17._____   27._____

8._____   18._____   28._____

9._____   19._____   29._____

10._____   20._____   30._____

Describe with Sensory Images

Directions: Choose one of the topics below, and then write a descriptive paragraph in the space provided. Use words or phrases that appeal to the five senses. For help, refer to the list of commonly used sensory words on the next page.

A School Cafeteria	**A Family Picnic**
The Beach	**A Family Reunion**
A Movie Theater	**An Amusement Park**
A Football or Baseball Game	**A School Gymnasium**
A Favorite Restaurant	**A Concert**

_____

_____

_____

_____

_____

_____

_____

_____

_____

_____

_____

_____

Sensory Word Picture Scavenger Hunt

1. Cut out 15 of the 45 sensory words below.
2. Cut out a picture from a magazine or newspaper that represents each sensory word.
3. Glue pictures on a piece of construction paper. Above each picture, glue the appropriate sensory word.

Taste	Touch	Smell	Sound	Sight
bitter	sticky	fresh	boom	huge
chewy	furry	smoky	ring	round
gritty	smooth	musty	click	flat
creamy	slippery	moldy	tick-tock	straight
salty	slimy	lemony	roar	twisted
spicy	sandy	fishy	splash	curved
sweet	icy	pungent	whisper	dark
lumpy	soft	stinky	hiss	bright
hot	rough	sweet	bang	multi-colored

Elaborate with Sensory Images, Examples and an Anecdote

Directions: Choose another topic from page 42 and write a paragraph, using sensory words, examples, and an anecdote. Refer to the guidelines at the bottom of this page for help.

_____

_____

_____

_____

_____

_____

_____

_____

_____

_____

_____

_____

- Clearly state the main idea of your paragraph in the topic sentence.
- Support your main idea with at least three examples.
- Include a strongly supportive anecdote that has a beginning, middle, and end.
- Use sensory words throughout the paragraph.
- End your paragraph with a concluding sentence that restates the main idea.

Elaborate with Quotes and Dialogue

Quoting someone and/or using dialogue are other ways to elaborate on your main idea. When used correctly, quotes and dialogue lend support to your statements.

Directions: Read the paragraphs below and notice how the quotes make them more inviting to read.

"Young lady, your shorts are way too short!" yells Mrs. Smith, our assistant principal.

As she escorts you into her office, you cry, "I'm sorry, but I woke up late this morning, so I grabbed the first thing I saw. Please don't call my dad."

Have you ever found yourself in this same predicament? Wearing school uniforms would eliminate wardrobe decisions in the morning and most importantly, eliminate dress code referrals to the assistant principal. Students, teachers, and administrators would all benefit from a mandatory school uniform.

"I consider myself very fortunate to have found such a responsible and trustworthy babysitter for my twin boys." "Bobby really knows how to handle my kids, and he sees to it that my 'To Do' list is completed before I arrive home from work." These are just two of the comments made by parents who have hired me as their babysitter for years. When searching for a qualified babysitter, most parents look for certain qualities like trustworthiness, responsibility, and experience. I possess these qualities, as well as a love for children that really shines through. I always furnish letters of recommendation with comments such as those above, to parents who are looking for the ideal babysitter.

Elaborate with Quotes, Dialogue, Examples, and an Anecdote

Directions: Read the elaborated paragraph below. Note how quotes, dialogue, examples, and an anecdote all combine to make an elaborated paragraph that is both interesting and convincing. Underline the anecdote.

"Oh my gosh! Look at what that girl is wearing today."

"Those yellow overalls are so ugly. I would never be seen in public wearing an outfit like that."

"That girl has no taste in clothes."

Unfortunately, conversations like this are pretty normal at my school, where people are judged by what they wear and how they look. This is so unfair because we all can't afford stylish clothes. School uniforms would put an end to these mean comments and take enormous pressure off of all of us. Wearing uniforms, we're all on the same level. Even those who can afford stylish and expensive clothes from The Gap or Express wouldn't feel the pressure of wearing a new outfit every day. In addition, parents would be relieved of a great financial burden all year long. Last year, our school sent out letters to parents asking them to vote on school uniforms. My dad said, "Uniforms are the answer to one of the main problems facing students every day."

My mom went so far as to say, "I wouldn't mind wearing a uniform to work myself."

As you can see, both parents and teens would benefit from school uniforms.

I admire my mom because she is so generous with my friends. Whenever I have a sleepover, she magically changes into some sort of genie who grants my every wish and waits on my friends and me hand-and-foot. I can almost hear her now. "What can I get for you girls to drink?" Or she might ask, "What would you like for dinner tonight? Do you want to order pizza or go out for hamburgers?" If she sees us getting bored later in the evening, she'll ask if we would like to rent some movies. I remember just two weeks ago, I had a sleepover at my house and invited four of my friends. After we had eaten dinner, Mom asked, "Who wants to go out for hot fudge sundaes? It's my treat."

Everyone cried, "Yes!"

That evening, one of my friends called her "Best All-Around Mom." That really made her feel special. I consider myself lucky to have such a giving mom. She really knows how to relate to teenagers.

Elaborate with Quotes, Dialogue, Examples, and an Anecdote *(cont.)*

Directions: You have read two examples of paragraphs using quotes and/or dialogue. Now it's your turn to write an elaborated paragraph on the topic below. Don't forget to use examples, an anecdote, and quotes and/or dialogue. Write your paragraph on the space provided below. Refer to the guidelines at the bottom of this page for help.

Topic: Think about a trait that you admire in a present or former teacher. Refer to page 37 for ideas. Now write an elaborated paragraph explaining why you admire this particular teacher.

_____

_____

_____

_____

_____

_____

_____

_____

- Clearly state the main idea of your paragraph in the topic sentence.
- Support your main idea with at least three examples. Don't forget to use vivid adjectives.
- Include a strongly supportive anecdote that has a beginning, middle, and end.
- Use quotes and/or dialogue.
- End your paragraph with a concluding sentence that restates your main idea.

Elaborate with Similes

Including comparisons and figurative language in your writing allows readers to more clearly see and understand the concepts and sensations that you are describing. The most common type of comparison is the simile. A simile compares two persons, places, or things by using the words "like" or "as."

Directions: Read the sentences below and then write down what two objects are being compared on the space provided. The first one has been done for you.

1. My mother is like a genie granting our every wish.

   mother—genie

2. Her hands were like butterflies fluttering across the keyboard.

   _____

3. From an airplane, people look like a bunch of ants traveling across land.

   _____

4. I jumped like a startled jackrabbit when the doorbell rang.

   _____

5. My words came back to haunt me like a boomerang returning to its thrower.

   _____

6. She was as pleased as a dog who has discovered a favorite bone.

   _____

7. No insults can hurt me, because my self-esteem is as hard as steel.

   _____

8. I fell like a thunderbolt when his punch struck the side of my face.

   _____

9. He reacted to the surprise party like a person who has just won the lottery.

   _____

10. When I entered the dark cave, I felt as solitary as a pearl in an oyster.

   _____

Spot the Simile

Directions: Read the elaborated paragraphs below. Find the similes and underline them.

Being a member of a gang spells nothing but "trouble," guaranteeing a life of crime and violence. First of all, to be inducted into a gang, a person usually has to go through some painful ritual and must commit a violent and criminal act. To stay in a gang, a member must continue to perform violent and illegal acts. A person's life changes, as does his/her personality. I remember a kid in seventh grade who got involved with a street gang. He used to be a likeable, peaceful, and kind-hearted person. Now, Tony is like a heartless, brutal machine with no regard for human life. He's always in trouble at school because he tries to "bully" everybody around. He was suspended three times for starting fights and expelled this year for hitting a teacher. Gangs are "bad news," and no one in his right mind should ever get involved with them.

People all over this country complain about being "stressed-out." Pressures from home and the workplace continue to mount as competition for job promotions and higher salaries increases. Doctors prescribe tranquilizers or muscle relaxants for patients complaining of stress; however, not everyone wants to take such drugs.  As an alternative, making time for a relaxing massage has become a popular treatment for many Americans. A stiff neck and tense shoulders, overused or extended muscles, and endless headaches find relief on the massage table. The masseur's advertisement in the local yellow pages reads, "Come in for a massage. You'll come out purring like a kitten." With the help of skilled massage therapists, Americans can finally be on the winning side of the fight against stress.

Elaborate with Facts and Statistics

> Adding facts and statistics to your writing will make your paragraphs much stronger. They offer supporting evidence, whether you are stating an opinion or offering a solution to a problem.

A <u>fact</u> is a statement that can be proven.
Example: George Washington was the first president of the United States.
A <u>statistic</u> is a fact stated in numbers.
Example: More than 58,000 Americans died in the Vietnam War.

Directions: Read the items below, then underline the facts and statistics that offer support for the author's opinion.

A. I believe that foreign countries should settle their own differences. The struggle between North and South Vietnam should have been fought by the citizens of those countries. They lived there, so they should have been the ones to give up their lives for their country. More than 58,000 Americans died in that war, and about 300,000 were wounded and disabled. Many American soldiers are still MIA—missing in action. They have never been found. The United States paid a high price for a conflict that was none of our business. This must not happen again.

B. Americans today are living longer lives than their ancestors. In 1970, 8% of all Americans were over 65 years old. By 1990, that figure rose to 12%. In the year 2000, people over 65 made up 20% of the population. As you can see, Americans can now look forward to increasingly longer lives.

C. Depression is prevalent among American teens today. Over two million young people suffer from some form of depression, but only 40% of them seek medical or professional attention. As a matter of fact, their depression often goes undetected by schools and family members. Nearly 75% of those who do receive initial treatment do not recover because they stop going to counseling or quit taking their medication. Without treatment and further counseling, these depressed teens grow to adulthood as unhappy, dysfunctional adults. Teen depression is an emotional disorder which must be recognized and treated conscientiously if teens are to lead normal and productive lives.

Spot the Facts and Statistics

Directions: The elaborated paragraph below uses facts and statistics to help support the main idea. The topic sentence has been underlined for you. Circle the facts and statistics that support this main idea.

As my grandparents gave me my own horse for my 14th birthday, I believe that my parents should allow me to work at a part-time job. The cost of caring for Rex, my thoroughbred Palomino, is extremely expensive, so I need to earn extra money. Birthday money, Christmas money, and my allowance simply aren't enough to cover Rex's expenses. Besides spending $20.00 a week on oats and hay, I must also pay for costly visits to the veterinarian which can cost between $200 and $500 a year. Rex's vitamins are $15.00 a month, and the cost for keeping him at the stables is $35.00 per month. In addition, I intend to train him to be a show horse. Training lessons for show horses can cost anywhere from $30.00 to $40.00 per lesson. Rex means a lot to me, and I want to do whatever it takes to keep him. Getting a part-time job is the only solution to my dilemma.

Athletes have been taking performance-enhancing substances for many centuries. However, it wasn't until the 20th century that the athletic world discovered a drug to create bigger and bulkier muscles—a drug that improves speed, power, and strength. This drug, known as steroids, was first developed by scientists in Germany during World War II. Its purpose was to make the German military more aggressive in battle. It wasn't until the 1950s that weight lifters in the United States and other countries began using and feeling the effects of steroids. A government report estimates that between 2 and 11 percent of high school athletes, 10 to 20 percent of college athletes, and 50 to 90 percent of amateur body builders use steroids. Due to these alarming numbers, educational programs regulating steroid use and its effects were implemented in most American schools in the 1980s. Since then, athletes have been closely monitored and even disqualified from competitions if evidence of steroid use has been found. The fight against these drugs, which destroy the body and undermine fairness in competition, continues today.

Tips for Writing Effective Sentences

❑ **Vary the sentence structure.**

In order to avoid a monotonous style, vary the way that you begin each sentence. The following is a list of methods and examples to vary the sentence structure:

a. Begin with prepositional phrases.
example: The private investigator sat in the police car.
revised: In the police car sat the private investigator.

b. Begin with an adverb.
example: The principal proudly distributed the awards.
revised: Proudly, the principal distributed the awards.

c. Begin with an adverb clause.
example: James was not afraid to fight, although his opponent outweighed him.
revised: Although his opponent outweighed him, James was not afraid to fight.

d. Begin with a participal phrase.
example: The old man, plodding through the snow, reached the station.
revised: Plodding through the snow, the old man reached the station.

e. Begin with an infinitive phrase.
example: You must exercise every day to stay physically fit.
revised: To stay physically fit, you must exercise every day.

❑ **Combine short, choppy sentences.**

Short, choppy sentences make your essay sound mechanical. While sometimes effective, they tend to bore the reader. By combining some of your short, related sentences, you will make your essay more interesting. The following is a list of combining methods:

a. Insert adjectives and prepositional phrases appropriately to make an effective, longer sentence.
example: Jane wore a sweater to the family reunion.
The sweater was light blue.
revised: Jane wore a light-blue sweater to the family reunion.

b. Combine by constructing participal or appositive phrases.
example: The referee signaled a touchdown.
The referee was standing in the end zone.
revised: Standing in the end zone, the referee signaled a touchdown.
example: Jack won the spelling bee.
Jack is an excellent student.
revised: Jack, an excellent student, won the spelling bee.

Tips for Writing Effective Sentences *(cont.)*

    c. Use compound subjects, compound verbs, and compound sentences to repair a short, choppy style.

       example: I went to the University of Florida.

       My brother went to the University of Florida, too.

       revised: My brother and I went to the University of Florida.

       example: Dad repaired his sports car Saturday.

       Dad raced his sports car on Sunday.

       revised: Saturday, Dad repaired his sports car, and he raced it on Sunday.

    d. Combine short, related sentences into compound or complex sentences.

       example: The pitcher threw a fast ball. The batter hit a homer.

       revise d: The pitcher threw a fast ball, but the batter hit a homer.

❑ **Avoid repetition of words and/or phrases.**

Substitute pronouns and synonyms for key words in your essay. Reword key phrases when referring to an object or event mentioned earlier in the essay. The following are examples:

    example: Mrs. Jones gets up every day at 5:30 A.M. to run three miles so that Mrs. Jones can stay fit.

    revised: Mrs. Jones gets up every day at 5:30 A.M. to run three miles so that she can stay fit.

    example: The students worked together to produce a video of which the students could be proud.

    revised: The students worked together to produce a video of which they could be proud.

❑ **Avoid rambling sentences.**

When combining short, choppy sentences, avoid combining ideas that are too lengthy, stuck together with too many conjunctions including *and, or, but, so, yet*.

    example: Last night I saw a program and it was about the presidential debate and my younger sister had a temper tantrum, so Mom sent her to her room and told her she was on restriction for two weeks and that she had better change her attitude or she would be on restriction for a longer time next time.

    revised: Last night, while watching the presidential debate on television, my younger sister had a temper tantrum. Mom sent her to her room and restricted her for two weeks. If she doesn't change her attitude, her next restriction will be longer.

Scoring Elaborated Paragraphs

Directions: Carefully read over the model scoring key and characteristics of an eleborated paragraph below.

Scoring Key for Elaborated Paragraphs.

Excellent = (5)	Good = (4)	Fair = (3)	Poor = (2)	Unsatisfactory = (1)

Score	Characteristics of an Elaborated Paragraph
	Clarity of main idea (main idea is stated clearly)
	Related details (all details relate to the main idea)
	Supporting details (examples and details support the main idea)
	Use of an anecdote (anecdote has a beginning, middle, and end)
	Concluding sentence (last sentence brings the paragraph to a close)
	Vivid examples (strong verbs/adjectives, sensory images, exact nouns, similes)
	Quotes/dialogue, facts, and/or statistics
	Vocabulary appropriate to grade level
	Varied sentence structure (various sentence types are used)
	Satisfactory grammar, mechanics, and spelling
	Total Score
	Final Score (total score divided by 10)

See if you can incorporate these characteristics of an elaborated paragraph in your own writing.

Models of Elaborated Paragraphs

Directions: Now it is time to learn how to score an elaborated paragraph. Read the three paragraphs that follow. Each one has been scored on a scale of 1–5. One is the lowest score and 5 is the highest. Below each paragraph is a completed score sheet.

<u>Topic</u>: We are all familiar with the many billboards on U.S. highways. Some people believe that they should be removed while others disagree. What do you think? Explain your point of view.

We need billboards for many reasons. They tell you where McDonalds is and where to go to the bathroom. Some are really pretty and I'm sure cost a lot of money to make. We need something to do on our boring trips, so I vote for keeping billboards. They're great! I think road signs, like slippery or curved road coming up are important too. You could get into an accident without them warning you. Then you'd end up in the hospital or even dead. That would be horrible for you and your family. So vote to keep billboards on the highways.

Excellent = (5)	Good = (4)	Fair = (3)	Poor = (2)	Unsatisfactory = (1)

Score	Characteristics of an Elaborated Paragraph
2	Clarity of main idea (main idea is clear)
2	Related details (all details relate to the main idea)
2	Supporting details (examples and details support the main idea)
1	Use of an anecdote (anecdote has a beginning, middle, and end)
2	Concluding sentence (an ending sentence bringing the paragraph to an end)
2	Vivid examples (strong verbs/adjectives, sensory images, and similes)
1	Quotes/dialogue, facts, and/or statistics
2	Vocabulary appropriate to grade level
2	Sentence structure (a variety of sentence types are used)
3	Satisfactory grammar, mechanics, and spelling
19	Total Score
1.9	Final Score (total divided by 10)

Models of Elaborated Paragraphs *(cont.)*

Topic: Billboards

Would you like to drive along the highway with nothing to do? I certainly wouldn't. I am for keeping billboards and advertisements. They give you something to do rather than being bored the whole way to your destination. It's fun reading and looking at the different signs. Some tell you where to turn off for entertainment and restaurants. Others tell you about certain places to visit. Without these advertisements, I am positive that my family and I would have no fun on our road trips. I really think we should keep the billboards on the highways.

Excellent = (5)	Good = (4)	Fair = (3)	Poor = (2)	Unsatisfactory = (1)

Score	Characteristics of an Elaborated Paragraph
3	Clarity of main idea (main idea is clear)
3	Related details (all details relate to the main idea)
3	Supporting details (examples and details support the main idea)
1	Use of an anecdote (anecdote has a beginning, middle, and end)
3	Concluding sentence (an ending sentence bringing the paragraph to an end)
3	Vivid examples (strong verbs/adjectives, sensory images, and similes)
1	Quotes/dialogue, facts, and/or statistics
3	Vocabulary appropriate to grade level
3	Sentence structure (a variety of sentence types are used)
4	Satisfactory grammar, mechanics, and spelling
27	Total Score
2.7	Final Score (total divided by 10)

Models of Elaborated Paragraphs *(cont.)*

<u>Topic:</u> Billboards

When my family and I take vacations by car, we look for the exciting billboards along the highway. Billboards should be kept and maintained. Everyone in my family enjoys them and benefits from them. What interests me the most are advertisements about restaurants and where they are located. My dad is interested in signs with information on fuel prices and the exits to take to reach the gas station. I can hear him now telling my mom, "Edith, are you keeping an eye open for the cheapest gas station?" On one of our trips, I recall seeing a car that had run out of gasoline on the roadside; the driver obviously didn't pay attention to the billboards. I noticed that the driver was crying. My dad pulled over and assured her that we would stop at the next gas station exit and bring fuel back for her car. That would have never happened if she had been a more attentive driver. While traveling, Mom looks at billboards advertising motels with modest rates and swimming pools. Grandma searches for billboards advertising antique shops. My brother, Jimmy, can't read yet, but he recognizes the letters of the alphabet. When he becomes restless, we play a game called, "How Many Billboards Start with a Certain Letter?" Information and amusement are two excellent reasons for maintaining billboards on our highways. America wouldn't be the same without them.

Excellent = (5)	Good = (4)	Fair = (3)	Poor = (2)	Unsatisfactory = (1)

Score	Characteristics of an Elaborated Paragraph
5	Clarity of main idea (main idea is clear)
5	Related details (all details relate to the main idea)
5	Supporting details (examples and details support the main idea)
5	Use of an anecdote (anecdote has a beginning, middle, and end)
5	Concluding sentence (an ending sentence bringing the paragraph to an end)
5	Vivid examples (strong verbs/adjectives, sensory images, and similes)
5	Quotes/dialogue, facts, and/or statistics
5	Vocabulary appropriate to grade level
5	Sentence structure (a variety of sentence types are used)
5	Satisfactory grammar, mechanics, and spelling
50	Total Score
5.0	Final Score (total divided by 10)

Evaluating Elaborated Paragraphs

Directions: Read the three paragraphs that follow. Each one should be scored on a scale of 1 – 5; 1 is the lowest score, and 5 is the highest. Complete the scoresheet below each paragraph.

<u>Topic</u>: Everyone has a favorite television program. Which one is your favorite and why? Write an elaborated paragraph explaining your choice.

Everyone has a favorite television program. What is your favorite television program? Mine is *The Simpsons*, because it is so great. The reason I like it so much is because it's so funny and it makes me laugh all the time. Bart's sneaky ways or Homer's way of thinking are so weird. It seems that every once in a while one of the family members will say something stupid. My mom and dad say its stupid I like it a lot. You should watch it.

Excellent = (5)	Good = (4)	Fair = (3)	Poor = (2)	Unsatisfactory = (1)

Score	Characteristics of an Elaborated Paragraph
	Clarity of main idea (main idea is stated clearly)
	Related details (all details relate to the main idea)
	Supporting details (examples and details support the main idea)
	Use of an anecdote (anecdote has a beginning, middle, and end)
	Concluding sentence (last sentence brings the paragraph to a close)
	Vivid examples (strong verbs/adjectives, sensory images, exact nouns, similes)
	Quotes/dialogue, facts, and/or statistics
	Vocabulary appropriate to grade level
	Varied sentence structure (various sentence types are used)
	Satisfactory grammar, mechanics, and spelling
	Total Score
	Final Score (total score divided by 10)

Evaluating Elaborated Paragraphs *(cont.)*

<u>Topic</u>: Television Program

> Moesha is my favorite television program. I like it because Moesha seems to have the problems that we teenage girls have today. For example, there are girlfriends dealing with boyfriends who cheat on them, smoking or not smoking cigarettes or pot, and last but not least, whether or not to follow the popular crowds in everything they do. On this show, Moesha makes bad choices sometimes. But sometimes later on she pays the consequences for those bad choices. We teenagers have to make choices all the time and sometimes don't know what to do. After I look at this television show, I stop and think about some of my own actions and choices and what Moesha has done. I feel that I have learned a lot from watching this show and think all teenagers should watch and learn from it too.

Excellent = (5)	Good = (4)	Fair = (3)	Poor = (2)	Unsatisfactory = (1)

Score	Characteristics of an Elaborated Paragraph
	Clarity of main idea (main idea is clear)
	Related details (all details relate to the main idea)
	Supporting details (examples and details support the main idea)
	Use of an anecdote (anecdote has a beginning, middle, and end)
	Concluding sentence (an ending sentence bringing the paragraph to an end)
	Vivid examples (strong verbs/adjectives, sensory images, and similes)
	Quotes/dialogue, facts, and/or statistics
	Vocabulary appropriate to grade level
	Sentence structure (a variety of sentence types are used)
	Satisfactory grammar, mechanics, and spelling
	Total Score
	Final Score (total divided by 10)

Evaluating Elaborated Paragraphs *(cont.)*

<u>Topic:</u> Television Program

Though I have little time to watch television, I am compelled to tune in on Thursday nights to watch *Friends*, my favorite television program. It is rated as one of the top five TV programs in the United States. I can always count on the cast to make me laugh hysterically, sometimes to the point of tears, and to make me reflect on "real-life" problems that are normally pretty serious. Even my Mom said the other night, "This whole gang of friends manages to get into some unpredictable, but outrageously funny and entertaining situations." One particular show comes to mind. Two of the main characters break up and their friends agonize over which side to take. They spend almost the entire half-hour arguing over the differing points of view from each side. While the gang is still arguing, the couple gets back together again, but the friends are now in a fight. However, the viewer knows that everything will be all right again because *Friends* is like a merry-go-round; no matter what, the gang always ends up in the same spot—friends again. I can't resist making time for a television program that always makes me laugh and lifts my spirits. I hope it continues to air for a long time.

Excellent = (5)	Good = (4)	Fair = (3)	Poor = (2)	Unsatisfactory = (1)

Score	Characteristics of an Elaborated Paragraph
	Clarity of main idea (main idea is stated clearly)
	Related details (all details relate to the main idea)
	Supporting details (examples and details support the main idea)
	Use of an anecdote (anecdote has a beginning, middle, and end)
	Concluding sentence (last sentence brings the paragraph to a close)
	Vivid examples (strong verbs/adjectives, sensory images, exact nouns, similes)
	Quotes/dialogue, facts, and/or statistics
	Vocabulary appropriate to grade level
	Varied sentence structure (various sentence types are used)
	Satisfactory grammar, mechanics, and spelling
	Total Score
	Final Score (total score divided by 10)

Teaching Guide for Part Two— Writing Elaborate Essays

Objectives

- To use a "web list" with supporting points and details that focuses on one main idea
- To review elaboration techniques
- To introduce the three parts of an essay and their guidelines
- To identify and later use the elements of strong introductions and conclusions
- To use transition words or phrases to show how ideas are related and to take a reader smoothly from one sentence or one paragraph to another
- To develop essays through the application of elaboration techniques
- To explain expository and persuasive essays
- To read peer writing models in order to identify elaboration techniques and qualities of good writing
- To score peer writing models in order to understand criteria by which their own writing will be assessed
- To follow the criteria for writing expository and persuasive essays which include introductions, elaborated body paragraphs, and conclusions
- To use a checklist during the editing process

Instructions for Part Two

1. Enlarge, post, and introduce page 63, "Characteristics of Effective Elaborated Essays" and Page 64, "The Five-Paragraph Essay."

2. Enlarge, post and introduce the web list for a five-paragraph essay on page 65.

3. Together with your class, practice "brainstorming" various topics; reproduce this page as often as needed. Various topics and web lists to be completed follow on pages 66–78.

4. Introduce "Guidelines and Models for Writing Introductions," page 79.

5. Enlarge post and review page 80, "Elaborating Body Paragraphs."

6. Practice reading two essays and find elaboration in each one with pages 81–85.

7. Introduce "Using Transitions," page 86.

8. Introduce "Guidelines and Models for Writing Conclusions," page 87.

9. Read "Models of Elaborated Essays" that have been scored, page 89–96.

Teaching Guide for Part Two— Writing Elaborate Essays *(cont.)*

Instructions for Part Two *(cont.)*

10. Score models of elaborated essays with students, page 97–104.

11. Review remaining points on "Characteristics of Effective Elaborated Essays" poster on page 63.

12. Some eighth grade state writing assessments incorporate persuasive and expository writing prompts. Refer to pages 105–106 for writing tips on these two types of prompts.

13. Assist your students in writing their own essays. Use topics on page 107 or make up your own topics. Have students begin by creating a web list on page 108.

Characteristics of Effective Elaborated Essays

- ❑ The writer states the main idea and supporting points in the introduction of the essay.
- ❑ The essay contains coherence and unity; sentences are related, connected, and focused, and there are no extraneous sentences.
- ❑ The writer uses transitions between paragraphs and ideas.
- ❑ The writer uses examples and vivid details to elaborate upon the supporting points.
- ❑ The essay contains elaboration techniques such as quotes, sensory words, figurative language, facts, and statistics.
- ❑ The writer includes an anecdote with a beginning, middle, and end.
- ❑ The writer uses quotes and/or dialogue to make the essay more interesting.
- ❑ The conclusion brings the essay to a definite close.
- ❑ The writer uses vocabulary appropriate to grade level.
- ❑ Sentence structure is varied.
- ❑ The writer uses correct spelling, grammar, capitalization, and punctuation.

The Five-Paragraph Essay

You have read the characteristics of an effective elaborated essay. It is also important to know what each paragraph of an essay contains. This knowledge will provide an organizational pattern for you to follow when you are writing your own persuasive or expository essays. The information below provides a pattern for a five-paragraph essay. Carefully read it over and use it as a reference when you begin writing your essay.

Paragraph	Characteristic
1	Your "introduction" includes a clear statement of the main idea. Include two or three supporting points. Use one of the "grabber" techniques listed on page 79.
2 3 4	These "body paragraphs" develop the main idea. Each body paragraph develops one specific point or reason by elaborating on it. Elaborate by using the "elaboration" techniques listed on page 80. Include an anecdote in one of the body paragraphs.
5	Your "conclusion" clearly indicates the end of your essay. Summarize or restate your supporting points or reasons. Use one or more of the "concluding" techniques listed on page 87.
Remember that each body paragraph contains a topic sentence that states the main point of that paragraph and a concluding sentence that brings that paragraph to a definite close.	

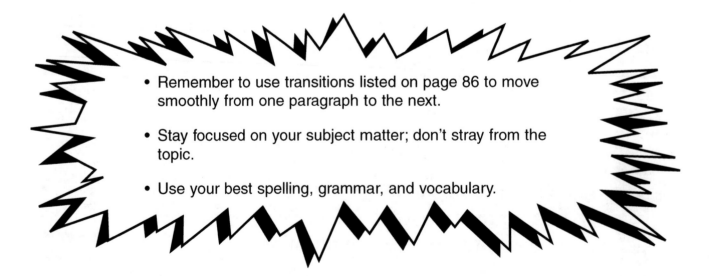

- Remember to use transitions listed on page 86 to move smoothly from one paragraph to the next.

- Stay focused on your subject matter; don't stray from the topic.

- Use your best spelling, grammar, and vocabulary.

Brainstorming for Ideas

Brainstorming is the foundation of a well-supported, elaborated essay. It is an essential part of the prewriting stage that organizes your essay. During this stage, you are exploring and jotting down ideas as they relate to your topic or thesis statement.

In the past, you have probably used one of two techniques, "clustering" or "listing." However, for the purpose of writing an elaborated essay, the diagram below is most beneficial. It is called a "web list." It reminds you to include three supporting points, several examples, and an anecdote in your essay.

Web List Diagram

Main Idea

supporting point

supporting point

examples

supporting point

examples

examples

1. _____
2. _____
3. _____
4. _____

1. _____
2. _____
3. _____

1. _____
2. _____
3. _____

Anecdote: _____

Models of a Web List

Study the web list below. It illustrates a combination of a cluster and a list of ideas related to the topic, "Qualities of a Good Friend."

Web List Diagram

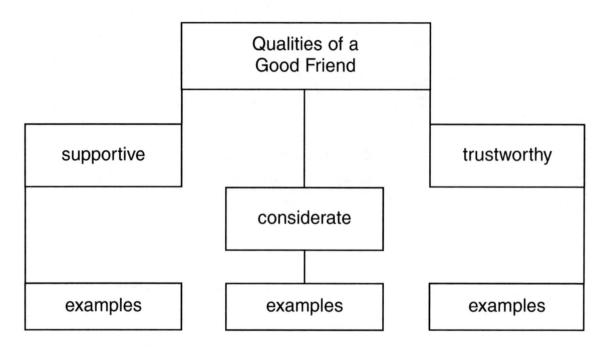

1. helps w/family

2. problems w/phone

3. problems w/boyfriend

1. gives me space

2. shares lunch sometimes

3. cheers me up when I am sick; get-well cards

1. returns borrowed things

2. keeps secrets

3. holds things for me

Anecdote: <u>fight between Mom and me about phone</u>

Models of a Web List *(cont.)*

Directions: Study the web list below and the one on the following page. Note how the one below, "The Driving Age Should Remain 16," has three supporting points. The web list on the following page, "How Watching Television Affects Grades," is supported by two points. Both should serve as future models for completing web lists.

Web List Diagram

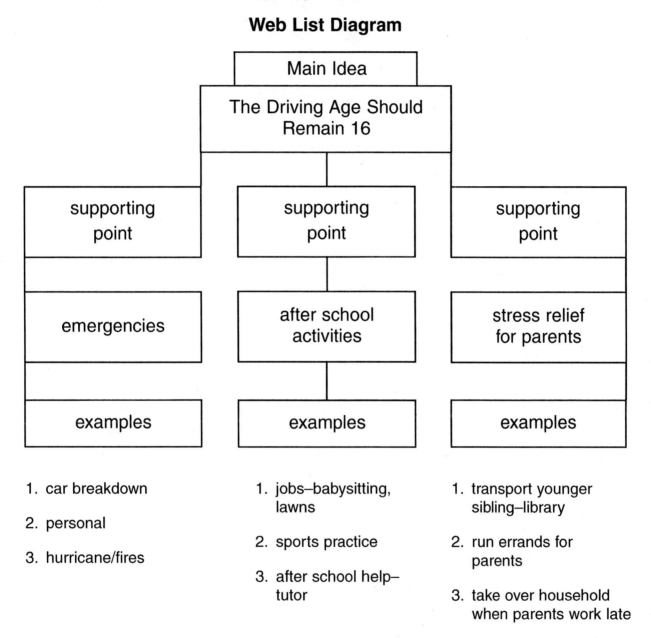

| Main Idea |
| The Driving Age Should Remain 16 |

supporting point	supporting point	supporting point
emergencies	after school activities	stress relief for parents
examples	examples	examples

1. car breakdown

2. personal

3. hurricane/fires

1. jobs–babysitting, lawns

2. sports practice

3. after school help–tutor

1. transport younger sibling–library

2. run errands for parents

3. take over household when parents work late

Anecdote: <u>Mom became ill, went to drugstore for prescriptions</u>

Models of a Web List *(cont.)*

Web List Diagram

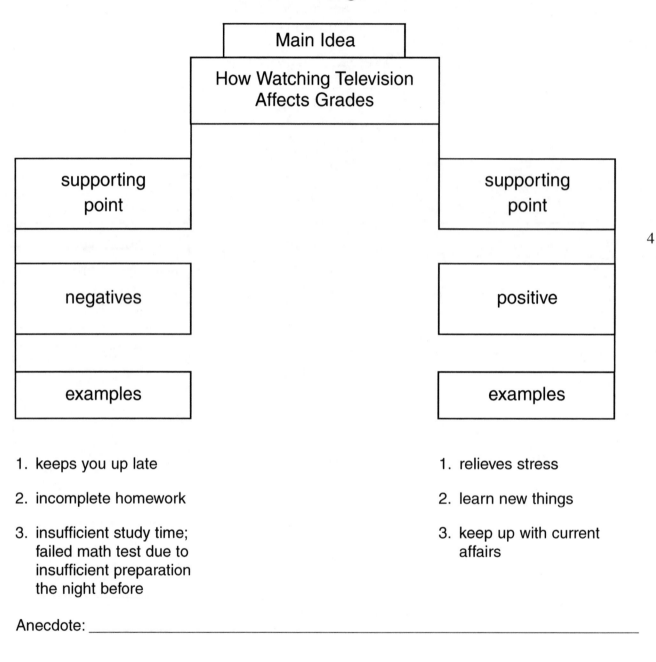

Main Idea

How Watching Television Affects Grades

supporting point

supporting point

4

negatives

positive

examples

examples

1. keeps you up late

2. incomplete homework

3. insufficient study time; failed math test due to insufficient preparation the night before

1. relieves stress

2. learn new things

3. keep up with current affairs

Anecdote: _____

_____

Complete the Web List

Directions: Examine the web lists below and on the following page. Notice that they are partially completed. Together with a group, brainstorm for ideas. Then, complete the web lists.

> Topic: Your school board is thinking about passing a new rule that all students should take a Red Cross health class. Write an essay convincing the school board to accept your point of view.

Web List Diagram

Main Idea
All students should take a Red Cross health class

supporting point	supporting point	supporting point
know first aid for camping	when people choke	
examples	examples	examples

1. snake bites	1. family picnics/reunions	1. _____
2. posion ivy	2. at restaurants	2. _____
3. sunburn	3. out to eat with friends	3. _____

Anecdote: <u>While camping with Boy Scouts, we cooked spoiled food; many had food poisoning</u>

Complete the Web List *(cont.)*

Topic: Complete the web list below for an essay explaining to your parents that you should have your own phone line.

Web List Diagram

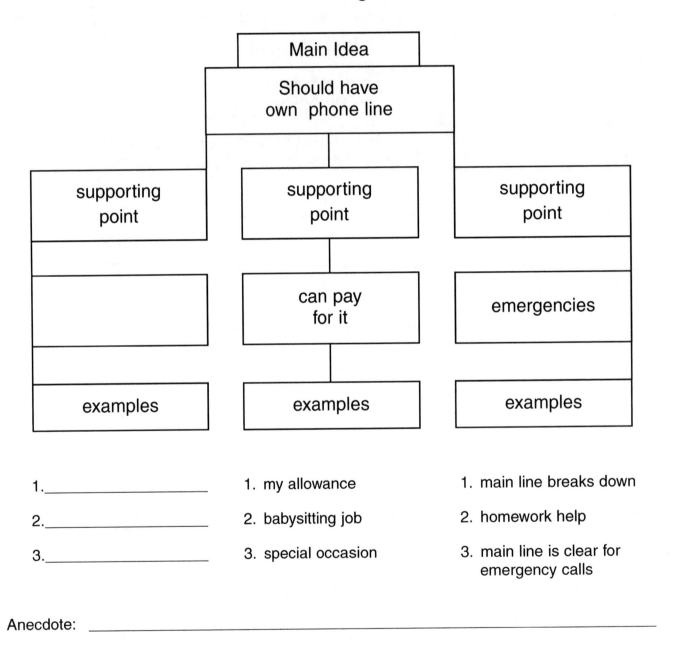

Main Idea

Should have own phone line

supporting point	supporting point	supporting point
	can pay for it	emergencies
examples	examples	examples

1._____	1. my allowance	1. main line breaks down
2._____	2. babysitting job	2. homework help
3._____	3. special occasion	3. main line is clear for emergency calls

Anecdote: _____

Construct a Web List

Directions: Now that you have had some practice examining and completing several web lists, it is your turn to construct a web list below and another on the following page.

<u>Topic</u>: Your community needs improvements. Think about one improvement for teens that would help the community. Write an essay explaining why you chose that improvement.

Web List Diagram

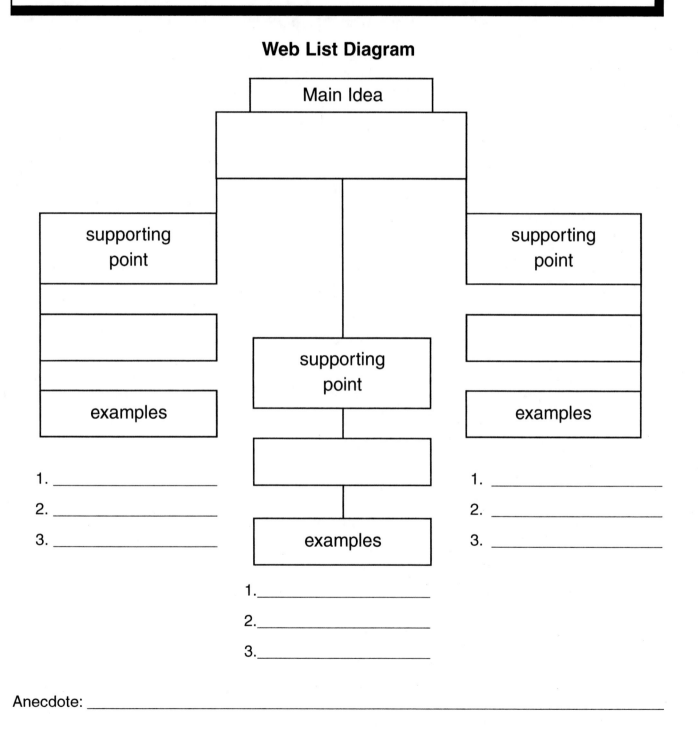

Anecdote: _____

Construct a Web List *(cont.)*

Directions: Carefully read the topic below and construct a web list.

Topic: There are five members in your household who use the same computer. You believe you should have your own. Write an essay persuading your parents that you should have your own computer.

Web List Diagram

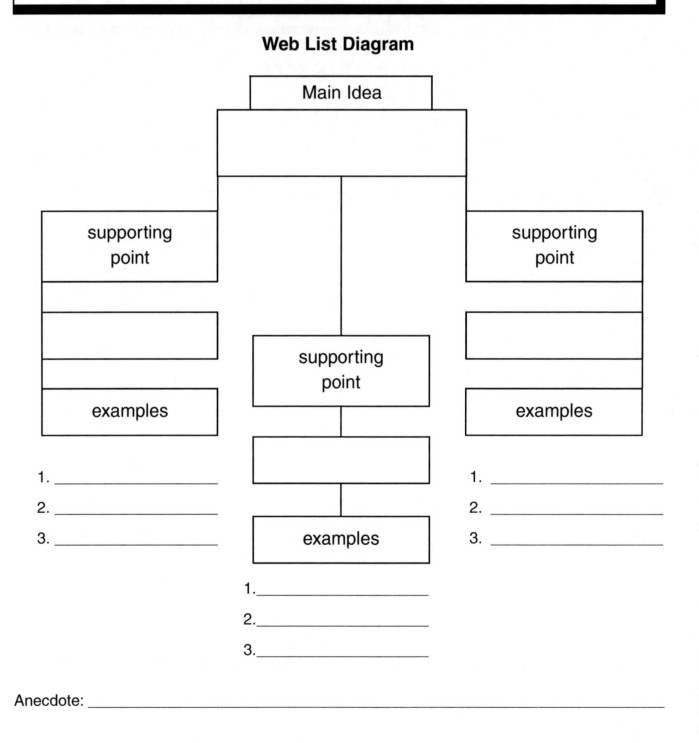

Anecdote: _____

Constructing a Web List from an Essay

Directions: Read the following two essays. Examine them for supporting points, examples, and an anecdote. Complete the web list that follows on page 75.

Topic: One of your best friends has started to smoke cigarettes. Write an essay convincing him/her that he/she should stop smoking.

"Just don't do it!" That's what I say to anyone who chooses to smoke cigarettes.

"Don't smoke around me. It's disgusting, and I hate the smell."

These are just some of the remarks I make to my friend, Bonnie. She just started smoking and doesn't seem to care about what anybody thinks. Not only does she appear to be blind to the harmful effects of smoking, but she also refuses to accept the fact that smoking causes poor hygiene and that she could be spending all that money on other more important things.

The major problem with smoking is that it does horrible and harmful things to your body. First of all, it is hazardous to your health because it is a major cause of lung cancer, heart disease, and other lung diseases. Statistics show that over two million Americans die every year of diseases related to cigarette smoking. Have you ever looked at the inside of a smoker's lungs? What you see is disgustingly black and tarry-looking. Have you ever been annoyed by a smoker's cough while sitting in a movie theater? Have you ever witnessed a smoker trying to run track or swim laps? When I pose these questions to Bonnie, she just gives me a snarly look in return.

Constructing a Web List
from an Essay *(cont.)*

(cont.)

Three years ago, someone very dear to me passed away from lung cancer. He was my grandfather. He started having problems at the age of 52, but was too stubborn to quit. Our entire family tried to convince him to stop; many of us begged him, but he didn't listen. Grandpa spent the last three weeks of his life in a hospital bed and in an oxygen tent before he died. He never got to see the birth of his first great grandson.

Yellow teeth, bad breath, and smelly clothes and hair are other negative effects of smoking cigarettes. Who wants to kiss a girl with smoker's breath? Who wants a photograph of a smoker with yellow teeth? Strong mouthwash, fragrant shampoo, and even whitening toothpaste won't change your appearance or improve bad breath. Looking and smelling bad detracts from a teen's looks, and no girl wants to look ugly in front of her friends.

Spending money on cigarettes is a complete waste. This money could be spent on the one thing girls never have enough of—clothes. Most girls agree that wearing stylish clothes and looking good in them makes them feel good. Also, if you spend your money on cigarettes, you won't even have enough to go out with your friends on the weekends. You can just say goodbye to movies, skating, and concerts. Your social life may come to an abrupt end, and you will probably lose some friends along the way.

In conclusion, I would like to say that I know this may have sounded like a lecture, but smoking is an emotional subject for me. I lost my grandfather to smoking, and I don't want to lose a friend too. Just remember that a lot of people care about what happens to you. Make the right choice for your life, your wealth, and most importantly, your health.

Constructing a Web List
from an Essay *(cont.)*

Web List Diagram

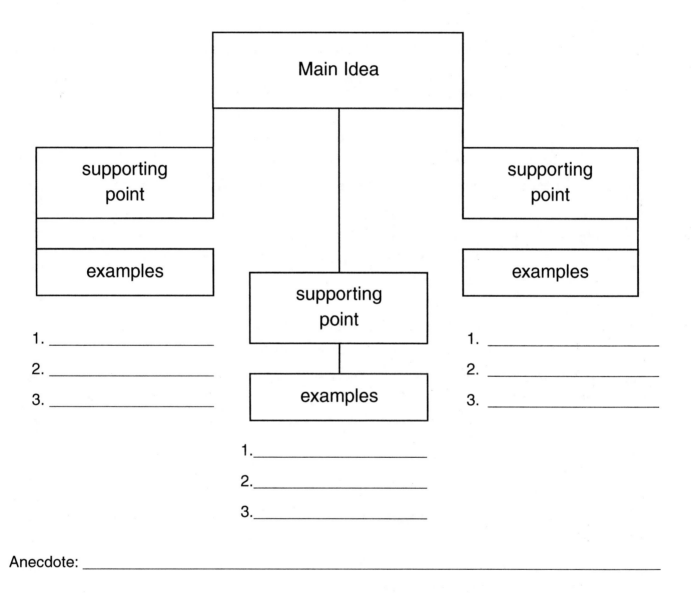

Anecdote: _____

Constructing a Web List
from an Essay (cont.)

Directions: This is the second essay that you will be examining for supporting points, examples, and an anecdote. Construct the web list that follows it.

Topic: You have been chosen by the mayor of your city to be his/her representative at your school. The mayor and the city council have passed a 10:00 P.M. teenage curfew law. Write an essay to your student body explaining the reasons for passing this law.

Every day on our local news channel, we hear two reoccurring themes regarding teenagers—reducing tragic auto accidents, usually drug- or alcohol-related, and raising state reading and math test scores. Our mayor and city council have passed a law that they believe will make our roads safer and will allow teens more study and homework time. This new law, which is a 10:00 P.M. weekday curfew for teens under 16, will be enacted next week.

It is no secret that most teens experiment with alcohol and/or drugs in high school. It is also no secret that drug dealers can be found by anyone, anywhere, anytime, but especially at night. The latest research shows us that 55% of all crimes take place late at night and that about 70% of all teen car accidents are either drug- or alcohol-related. The mayor wants us out of the streets for these very reasons. Our parents want us off the streets for our safety and well being. Just five months ago, a story about the deaths of two teenagers in our city was reported in our local newspaper, *The Tampa Tribune*. Two teens slipped out of their home, stole Dad's car, and went joyriding. Late into the night, their father reported them missing, and an alert with the car's description was sent out to the city police and highway patrol. Reportedly, around 1:00 A.M., a car fitting the description was spotted and chased by a police car. Despite the warning, the two teens accelerated their speed, spun around a corner, hit a telephone pole, and met their deaths. Do you want this to be you?

Constructing a Web List
from an Essay *(cont.)*

(cont.)

"No mom, I'll finish my homework and study for the test when I get back." Does this comment sound familiar? If you're like most teenagers, you have all kinds of after-school activities to take part in or you're with your friends late into the evening. Unfortunately, these weekday activities take away from precious study and homework time. As a result, fewer and fewer students achieve high honor roll, and our state reading tests show a decline in scores. It is time to take responsibility for our grades and to think seriously about our futures. Following the curfew and investing a little more time into studies now will surely pay off in the long run.

Please join me in helping our mayor, and especially teens, by staying off the streets after 10:00 P.M. Our parents will feel better knowing we are safe at home, and we will feel better about ourselves as we improve our test scores and "take a bite out of crime."

Constructing a Web List from an Essay *(cont.)*

Web List Diagram

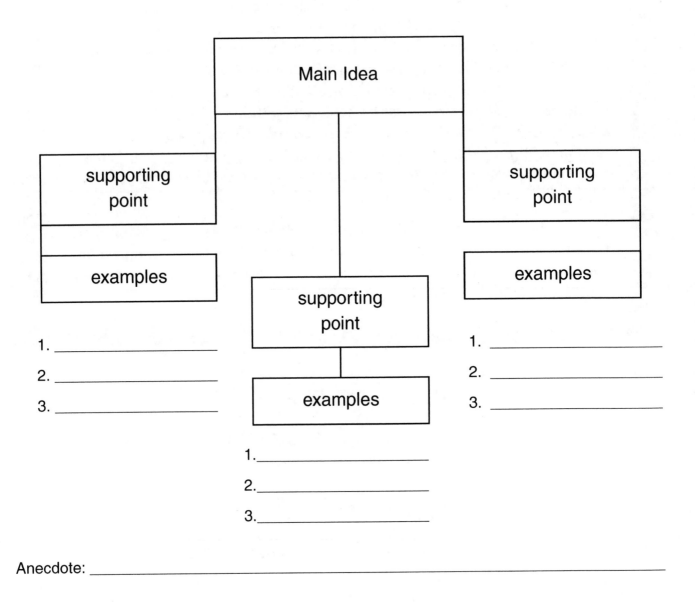

Anecdote: _____

Guidelines and Models for Writing Introductions

The introduction of your essay should be as attractive as a front cover of a book or the front door of a house. It should invite readers in by grabbing their attention immediately. An effective introduction sets the tone for the information to follow. There are several ways you can grab your reader's attention.

Below is a list of techniques for introductory paragraphs.

- Begin with an interesting quote, fact, or statistic.
- Begin with a thought-provoking question.
- Briefly describe an incident or conversation.
- Use humor—tell a joke or riddle.

Your introduction must include the following:

- A clear statement of the main idea of the essay; this is called a thesis statement.
- Two or three supporting points or reasons.
- One of the techniques listed above.

Directions: Read the two introductions below. The first one is weak; it does not clearly state the main idea and its two supporting points. It also does not include one of the introductory techniques listed above. The second revised introduction is stronger and more effective. It begins with an inviting quote and clearly states the main idea and supporting points.

I believe that I should be picked because I am a hard worker and I am dependable. If you ask me, I will do something. That's why I think that I should be picked because I will do what you want.

Mr. Principal, look no further. I'm the man for the job. I am confident in asking you to select me as one of your assistants because I was an office assistant for three years at my elementary school and because I am a dependable person. Experience and dependability make me an excellent choice for principal's assistant.

Elaborating Body Paragraphs

The paragraphs between the introduction and the conclusion are called the body paragraphs. These paragraphs develop the main idea by elaborating the supporting points. Each body paragraph elaborates one specific supporting point and should include as many elaboration techniques as possible. These elaboration techniques are covered and explained in Part One of this workbook.

A summary list of these techniques has been provided below. Remember that the effectiveness of your essay depends upon how well you develop your supporting points. Elaborate! Elaborate! Elaborate!

Elaboration Techniques

- Elaborate with Strong Verbs, Vivid Descriptive Adjectives, and Exact Nouns

- Elaborate by Expanding Sentences

- Elaborate with Examples

- Elaborate with Anecdotes

- Elaborate with Sensory Images

- Elaborate with Quotes/Dialogue

- Elaborate with Similes

- Elaborate with Facts and Statistics

similes

facts

examples

anecdotes

Spotting Elaboration Techniques

Directions: Read the two elaborated essays that follow. Examine them for elaboration techniques. Find words, phrases, or sentences that illustrate each of the elaboration techniques following the essays. Write them in the boxes provided on the next page.

The Ideal Babysitter

"Dependable" and "lovable" are words that describe me as the ideal babysitter for your children. Look no further; waste no more time. You have found your man.

A major trait to look for in a babysitter is dependability. Parents can depend on me to do all of the necessary chores a good babysitter should do: feed their kids (no chocolate-chip cookies before meals), bathe them before bedtime, and help school-aged children with homework and school projects. In addition, since safety is most important, parents can also rely on me not to open doors to strangers, not to have my friends come over while I'm babysitting, and not to let the children wander or play outside without my careful supervision.

Not long ago in our neighborhood, a two-year-old girl almost drowned in her swimming pool. The babysitter, who was talking on the phone with her boyfriend, didn't hear or see Stacey go outside and head for the pool. By accident, Stacey fell in. Had it not been for Rover's non-stop barking, the irresponsible sitter would have never reached Stacey in time to rescue her. Just yesterday, I heard on the news that about 2,000 American children every year drown or have a serious accident in their own backyard. That sort of accident would never happen if I were the babysitter.

People tell me I'm as devoted as a dog to children. Instead of talking on the phone with my friends or doing my own homework, I spend all of my time with the children I'm babysitting. I play their favorite games, do difficult puzzles, wrestle with the boys, and play "Barbies" with the girls. I guess you could say that I am really tuned-in to their needs.

The safety and loving care of your children are major priorities when you are looking for the right babysitter. I take these both very seriously and have the experience and parent recommendations to back me up. When it comes to ideal babysitters, I believe that I am a top pick.

Spotting Elaboration Techniques *(cont.)*

Techniques	Examples
vivid verbs	
vivid adjectives	
examples supporting main points or reasons	
anecdote	
quotes/dialogue	
similes	
sensory words/phrases	
facts/statistics	

Spotting Elaboration Techniques *(cont.)*

The Greatest Experience of My Life

One of the greatest and most exhilarating experiences of my life was when I rode a roller coaster for the first time. It was the most fun I had ever had, and I finally overcame my fear of riding roller coasters forever.

First and foremost, I have always been deathly afraid of riding roller coasters. On field trips with my classmates, I would always be the one left behind, holding purses and souvenirs for my friends while they rode the roller coasters and all the other dangerous rides. My fears included falling out or becoming unstrapped, something going wrong with the loud and powerful engine, or even the coaster slipping off its narrow, steep tracks and slamming into the ground below. One day in sixth grade, my best friend Mia challenged me to ride the "Python" with her at Busch Gardens. She said, "Erika, I'll ride it by myself, so you can see that it's not scary or dangerous at all." As I watched Mia riding the roller coaster alone, my stomach felt as though it was tied into a thousand knots. When the ride was over, Mia came from behind and grabbed me. Before I realized it, I was strapped in and on my way up. After about three minutes of the most awesome fun I had ever had, the ride came to an end and I found myself waiting in line again. Thanks to Mia, I'll never again be afraid of roller coasters.

Nothing is more exciting to me now than riding the wild loops and sharp turns of modern-day roller coasters. Sixty, seventy, and even eighty mile-per-hour speeds make the rides more thrilling and challenging than ever before. I feel like I am master of the universe as the brisk wind blows on my face and the next plunging dip comes into view. Being flipped upside down and turned and twisted from side to side doesn't even bother me anymore. As the coaster approaches its final twists and turns, I find myself yelling to my friends, "Let's ride it again!"

Riding a roller coaster for the first time was the biggest adventure of my life, and I shall always remember it. I'll never understand how something so-o-o scary can be so-o-o much fun!!!

Spotting Elaboration Techniques *(cont.)*

Techniques	Examples
vivid verbs	
vivid adjectives	
examples supporting main points or reasons	
anecdote	
quotes/dialogue	
similes	
sensory words/phrases	
facts/statistics	

Elaborating Body Paragraphs

Directions: Read the two body paragraphs below. Both build around one main idea. The writer claims to be a responsible person. Paragraph A is very weak because it has no elaboration. It has been revised in Paragraph B with the addition of several examples, an anecdote, and a quote. You should use Paragraph B as a model for elaboration.

Paragraph A

I believe that I am a responsible person. I am responsible with money and other chores at home. I am also responsible for arriving home and to other places on time. As you can see, I am really a very responsible person.

Paragraph B

I believe that I am a highly responsible thirteen-year-old. I arrive to school on time, arrive home ten minutes before curfew, and always complete my household chores on time. In addition, unlike my twin brother, I am extremely responsible with money. I remember one time when Mom gave my brother and me $25.00 each to spend on lunch and the arcade at the mall. About 15 minutes after we arrived, my brother lost his money. He spent most of his time looking for it, but never found it. I, on the other hand, played video games, ate pizza and ice cream, and still had money left in my pocket when we arrived home. I can still hear Mom yelling at him, "Why can't you be more responsible like your brother?" Being responsible has made my parents trust me more, which will come in handy when I turn sixteen and want to borrow the car.

Using Transitions

Body paragraphs should be organized in such a way that each sentence relates to the other sentences. Using transition words and phrases helps the reader clearly understand how one sentence relates to the other. Transitions also help the reader make the connection from one paragraph to the next. As a result, transition words and phrases keep the writing smooth and give it continuity.

Transition words and phrases for use in different parts of your essay are listed below. Note that some are repeated; they are appropriate for use in more than one part of your essay.

Transitions Used Within Paragraphs	Transitions Used from One Paragraph to the Next
• therefore • however • furthermore • then • next/following • in addition/also • in contrast • similarly	• first/to begin with/for one thing • second/secondly • lastly/finally • furthermore • following/in addition • equally important • thus
Transitions for Examples	**Transitions to Begin Anecdotes**
• for example • for instance • to illustrate • in particular	• on one occasion • one incident comes to mind • I recollect/I remember
Transitions to Begin Conclusions	
• in conclusion • to conclude • for those reasons • on the whole • as you can see • as stated above • therefore	

Guidelines and Models for Writing Conclusions

The conclusion of your essay clearly brings your essay to a definite close and completes the purpose of your essay. An effective conclusion leaves the reader thinking about what you have written. There are several ways that you can accomplish this.

Study the list of concluding techniques below.

- End with a thought-provoking question.
- End with a personal conclusion you have reached about the topic.
- End with a possible solution for a problem you've brought up in your essay.
- End with a comment that invites the reader to consider your point of view.

Your conclusion must include the following:

- a restatement of the main idea
- a summary of the main points
- one or two of the concluding techniques mentioned above

* New information should not be included in your closing.

Directions: Read the two conclusions below. The first one is weak and does not include a concluding technique. Note how the writer of the second paragraph has used a quote from his mother to create a more effective conclusion.

That is why I believe I should be a principal's assistant at my school. I am a hard worker and I am dependable as I have demonstrated.

Being a dependable person and working hard at whatever I do are two traits that my Mom instilled in me as a very young schoolboy. I can hear her words ringing in my ears: "Jason, work hard and be proud of everything you do. For this, people will come to respect you and depend upon you." I continue to practice those words that Mom preached, and I believe my dedication will make me a winner as a principal's assistant.

Scoring Elaborated Essays

Directions: Carefully read over the scoring sheet below.

Scoring Key for Elaborated Essays

Excellent = (5)	Good = (4)	Fair = (3)	Poor = (2)	Unsatisfactory = (1)

Score	Characteristics of an Elaborated Essay
	Clearly stated main idea in the introduction
	Introduction, Body Paragraphs, Conclusion
	Two or three clearly stated supporting points or reasons
	Vivid examples/details/sensory images
	One elaborated paragraph with anecdote
	Smooth transition from paragraph to paragraph
	Satisfactory grammar, spelling, and punctuation
	Varied sentence structure
	Age appropriate vocabulary
	No sentences off topic
	Total Score
	Final Score (total divided by 10)

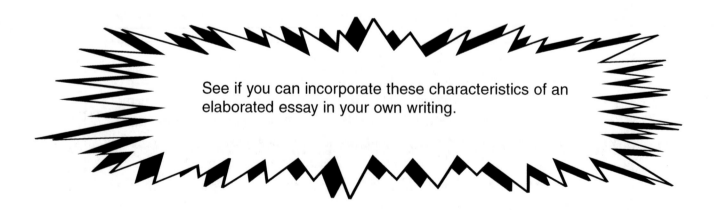

See if you can incorporate these characteristics of an elaborated essay in your own writing.

Models of Elaborated Essays

Directions: Carefully read the essays and the completed scoring keys that follow. Be sure to note the differences among them. The ones that scored a 4.9 or a 5 should be your models.

Topic: Many of us have wondered what it would be like to trade places with someone for a day. If given that choice, with whom would you like to change places? Explain your choice in an essay.

Trading Places with Someone for a Day

"Tony, may I leave an hour earlier today? I have a doctor's appointment."

"May I go to lunch now? I'm starving!"

These are just some of the questions that my older brother Tony has to answer throughout his workday. Making a decision about trading places with someone for a day would be very easy for me. Without hesitation, I would choose my brother Tony. To begin with, he has two fabulous jobs—one as a model and another as a store manager. He also has a driver's license, so he drives himself anywhere he wants to go. Tony is my idol, and I would love to experience his lifestyle.

More than anything, I would like to experience Tony's part-time job as a high-profile model. Modeling for a popular department store, he earns a good salary and enjoys great benefits for just showing up and letting photographers take pictures of him. If I were to trade places with my brother for a day, I'd be photographed in stylish and expensive outfits by professional photographers. Last summer, Tony was flown to an island in the Caribbean where he was photographed, modeling a variety of swim wear. The shoot took place by the pool in a luxurious, tropical hotel. After work, he and the rest of the crew toured the island and experienced the exciting night life of clubs and casinos. The modeling company paid for all of Tony's expenses for one whole week while he had nothing but fun. Give me a day like that to remember!

Unlike Tony, who is 26 years old, I am not allowed to drive a car and go places whenever I want to. However, for that one day that he and I do trade places, I would drive myself to work, meet friends for lunch, and then have the best evening of my life going to different dance clubs with my friends; of course, I would have no curfew either. Driving Tony's car for 24 hours would make me feel really independent and grown-up.

Models of Elaborated Essays *(cont.)*

(cont.)

As part-time manager of my mom's manicure and massage salon, Tony gets to tell the employees what to do. I would love to experience that feeling of being "the boss" and making decisions such as when an employee can go to lunch or receive a pay raise. In addition, Tony is highly respected and well liked by his staff. I would like to experience that too.

Spending Tony's money for a day would be a fabulous treat for me since my weekly allowance is a mere $10.00. If I had his income, I would buy anything I wanted from The Gap or J. Crew; I would also put Blockbuster Music on my list of places to shop. Living Tony's life would be like living in a fantasy.

As you can see, my brother's life is filled with excitement, glamour, money, and fun. I would consider myself very lucky to walk in his shoes for 24 hours. In the meantime, I'll just have to settle for dreaming about it.

Excellent = (5)	Good = (4)	Fair = (3)	Poor = (2)	Unsatisfactory = (1)

Score	Characteristics of an Elaborated Essay
5	Clearly stated main idea in the introduction
5	Introduction, Body Paragraphs, Conclusion
5	Two or three clearly stated supporting points or reasons
4	Vivid examples/details/sensory images
5	One elaborated paragraph with anecdote
5	Smooth transition from paragraph to paragraph
5	Satisfactory grammar, spelling, and punctuation
5	Varied sentence structure
5	Age appropriate vocabulary
5	No sentences off topic
49	Total Score
4.9	Final Score (total divided by 10)

Models of Elaborated Essays *(cont.)*

Topic: Trading Places with Someone for a Day

If I could trade places with someone for a day, it would have to be my mother. My mom is the most awesome person I know. She is a pediatric nurse, a great mom, and a great friend.

First of all, my mom takes care of newborn babies and premature babies at Women's Hospital. She works 12-hour shifts and is very tired when she gets home. Most of the babies that she takes care of are fine, but sometimes they are born sick. That is really sad.

My second reason for picking my mom is that she is the best parent in the world. She takes really good care of her three kids and gives us almost anything we want. She also lets us have friends over whenever we want. She is so cool.

My last reason for picking my mom is that she is my best friend. I can tell her about anything. Like one time I told her how upset I was that the boy I liked at school liked someone else. Most girls can't talk to their moms like that. We like to go rollerblading together too. However, mom doesn't have much time these days.

My mom is the best mom ever. I wish everybody could have a mom like mine.

Excellent = (5)	Good = (4)	Fair = (3)	Poor = (2)	Unsatisfactory = (1)

Score	Characteristics of an Elaborated Essay
3	Clearly stated main idea in the introduction
3	Introduction, Body Paragraphs, Conclusion
3	Two or three clearly stated supporting points or reasons
3	Vivid examples/details/sensory images
3	One elaborated paragraph with anecdote
3	Smooth transition from paragraph to paragraph
3	Satisfactory grammar, spelling, and punctuation
3	Varied sentence structure
3	Age appropriate vocabulary
4	No sentences off-topic
31	Total Score
3.1	Final Score (total divided by 10)

Models of Elaborated Essays *(cont.)*

I wish that I could trade places with Mr. Trumble for a day. He is my school principal. He is the boss of the school. He is everybody's boss. I want to be the boss for a day.

Mr. Trumble tells everybody what to do. He tells the teachers, the secretaries, and the helpers what to do. And they better listen. He makes rules for all the kids and they must obey them or get in trouble and maybe get suspended. He can also fire the teachers if they don't listen to him. And last of all, he is in charge of the buildings—air conditioning and the plants and whatever needs fixing. He wants the school to look good. That's why I want to be Mr. Trumble.

Excellent = (5)	Good = (4)	Fair = (3)	Poor = (2)	Unsatisfactory = (1)

Score	Characteristics of an Elaborated Essay
2	Clearly stated main idea in the introduction
1	Introduction, Body Paragraphs, Conclusion
1	Two or three clearly stated supporting points or reasons
1	Vivid examples/details/sensory images
1	One elaborated paragraph with anecdote
2	Smooth transition from paragraph to paragraph
3	Satisfactory grammar, spelling, and punctuation
1	Varied sentence structure
3	Age appropriate vocabulary
3	No sentences off-topic
18	Total Score
1.8	Final Score (total divided by 10)

Models of Elaborated Essays *(cont.)*

<u>Topic</u>: During the school year, most students have a favorite class. What is or was your favorite class? Write an elaborated essay about your favorite class.

My Favorite Class

Out of all of my classes, Spanish is my favorite. I admit that it isn't the usual academic math, science, or social studies class because it is an elective. But for me, there is a joy in learning Spanish that I just don't experience in my other classes. Maybe it's my interest in the Spanish culture, or maybe it is the Spanish teacher herself who makes this class "numero uno."

As I walk into the potpourri-scented classroom decorated with daisy-colored curtains and pictures of Spain, I am overcome by my curiosity to learn more about the culture. Sometimes I feel like a sponge, absorbing everything my teacher has to offer. For example, I learned that the elders of Spain are deeply respected and counted upon for their endless wisdom. Small children are included in adult activities such as weddings, parties, and religious celebrations. Taking an afternoon break, a siesta, and eating dinner around 9:00 p.m. are some other cultural traditions enjoyed by the Spanish.

My Spanish class has seen many videos of this beautiful country, and we have even watched Spanish soap operas. It was so much fun trying to figure out what the plot was and what the characters were saying. Learning the language and learning about the Spanish culture have been exciting.

"Buenos dias, clase. Como estan ustedes?" "Good day, class. How are you today?" This is how our teacher Mrs. Santiago greets us every day. She is a great teacher, one with a terrific sense of humor. She likes to act out roles in order to get her point across. We students sit in class, dazzled by her amazing stories and her amateur, but entertaining, performances. What a unique way she has in teaching a foreign language! Actually, we never know when she's going to pull something new on us. Last week, while teaching about Spanish folklore and folkdances, Mrs. Santiago turned on some Latin music and started dancing around the room. We all joined in and had a blast. Can't you just picture this 60-year-old lady, a little on the heavy side, "letting her hair down" in front of a bunch of teens? Awesome!

No other class can compare to my Spanish class. All of my other classes seem boring and colorless by comparison. The kind of excitement that Mrs. Santiago stirs up in her students and the "hands-on" learning she provides us with make this an A+ course. Muchas gracias, Señora Santiago.

Models of Elaborated Essays *(cont.)*

Excellent = (5)	Good = (4)	Fair = (3)	Poor = (2)	Unsatisfactory = (1)

Score	Characteristics of an Elaborated Essay
5	Clearly stated main idea in the introduction
5	Introduction, Body Paragraphs, Conclusion
5	Two or three clearly stated supporting points or reasons
5	Vivid examples/details/sensory images
5	One elaborated paragraph with anecdote
5	Smooth transition from paragraph to paragraph
5	Satisfactory grammar, spelling, and punctuation
5	Varied sentence structure
5	Age appropriate vocabulary
5	No sentences off-topic
50	Total Score
5	Final Score (total divided by 10)

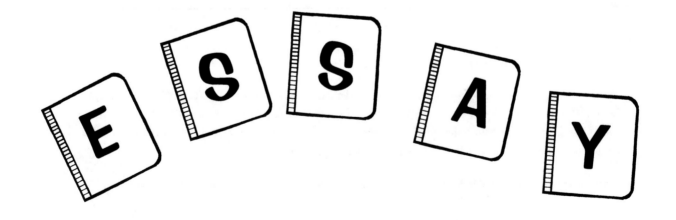

Models of Elaborated Essays *(cont.)*

<u>Topic</u>: My Favorite Class

All students have a favorite class and mine is physical education—P.E. You can do many things like exercise, run and socialize which are my three favorite things to do. Along with that you do other things, but those three are my favorites.

During P.E. you get lots of exercise. You play different kinds of games and have workouts, relays and other fun activities. For example, yesterday we played "capture the flag." It was so much fun and everyone had a good time.

The second reason P.E. is my favorite class is that I like to run. I am a fast runner and enjoy track and competition. Running is also good for you.

The third reason I like P.E. so much is because we get to socialize. You have many class discussions, work together in groups, and learn about how the body works. You also get to go on many field trips like roller skating, bowling, and amusement parks. My other classes are so boring and you don't get to go on field trips at all. You get to talk to your friends, too, in P.E. It's like not having a class.

That's why P.E. is my favorite class. Running, exercising, and socializing are my favorite things to do. I look forward to this class every day. Maybe someday I'll be a P.E. teacher.

Excellent = (5)	Good = (4)	Fair = (3)	Poor = (2)	Unsatisfactory = (1)

Score	Characteristics of an Elaborated Essay
4	Clearly stated main idea in the introduction
3	Introduction, Body Paragraphs, Conclusion
3	Two or three clearly stated supporting points or reasons
2	Vivid examples/details/sensory images
2	One elaborated paragraph with anecdote
3	Smooth transition from paragraph to paragraph
4	Satisfactory grammar, spelling, and punctuation
3	Varied sentence structure
3	Age appropriate vocabulary
3	No sentences off-topic
30	Total Score
3	Final Score (total divided by 10)

Models of Elaborated Essays *(cont.)*

Topic: My Favorite Class

My favorite class is TAP—Teacher Assisted Program. Everyday our teacher takes us to John Kennedy Elementary School to help the little kids. My friends and I love to go there.

I help the little kids learn how to read. I read all kinds of stories they really like. Reading is very important, and I want them to be good readers. They enjoy all of the stories I read to them and they ask me lots of questions at the end of the story. They're so cute.

It's a lot of fun being with little kids because I don't have any little brothers and sisters. They're so cute and funny and they ask a lot of silly questions.

I give them candy for being good and quiet while I am reading to them. They always beg for more. Chocolate candy is their favorite, but I give them different treats like cupcakes and popcorn too. TAP is my very favorite class.

Excellent = (5)	Good = (4)	Fair = (3)	Poor = (2)	Unsatisfactory = (1)

Score	Characteristics of an Elaborated Essay
2	Clearly stated main idea in the introduction
1	Introduction, Body Paragraphs, Conclusion
1	Two or three clearly stated supporting points or reasons
1	Vivid examples/details/sensory images
1	One elaborated paragraph with anecdote
2	Smooth transition from paragraph to paragraph
3	Satisfactory grammar, spelling, and punctuation
1	Varied sentence structure
3	Age appropriate vocabulary
2	No sentences off-topic
17	Total Score
1.7	Final Score (total divided by 10)

Evaluate Elaborated Essays

Directions: Read the essays that follow. Each one should be scored on a scale of 1–5; 1 is the lowest score, and 5 is the highest. Complete the scoresheet below each essay.

Topic: Your local school board is seriously thinking about school uniforms for all students in your district. What is you opinion? Write an essay convincing your school board to adopt or reject school uniforms.

"Uniforms! Absolutely not. We'll all look alike."

"What happened to individuality?"

These are just two of the comments you will be hearing from most 8th graders if school uniforms are imposed on us. Not me! I am in favor of school uniforms and I am ready to endorse them today for some very good reasons. First of all, there would be less peer pressure, fewer insults and criticisms, and definitely more carefree mornings.

Teens in America today face more peer pressure than ever before. We have enough to contend with when it comes to making decisions about drugs, alcohol, and belonging to the right crowd. Wearing designer clothes, shopping at the right department store and looking perfectly groomed are all pressures that burden students today. Not all of us can afford designer clothes. Not all of us look good in whatever style happens to be popular, and not all of us consider clothing to be the most important part of school. Therefore, make us all equal by making us all wear uniforms.

Now, for the mornings. I'm one of three teenage sisters, and mornings at my house are rather hectic. We can't always find what we want to wear because it's been borrowed, it's dirty, or it's been misplaced or lost. Consequently, we're fighting and very often arrive late to school. One eventful morning last winter comes to mind. I was getting ready to wear a gorgeous sky-blue sweater that I received for Christmas. I couldn't find it anywhere—not in my drawers, not in my closet, not in the laundry room and not even on the floor. I was so upset that I started screaming and crying so loud that my mom and dad rushed into my room to see what was wrong. After all three of us just about turned my room upside down searching for my new sweater, my older sister walked in and announced that she had borrowed it and taken it to the dry cleaners before returning it. Needless to say, I was furious

Evaluate Elaborated Essays *(cont.)*

and my morning was a complete disaster. That would never happen if we had to wear uniforms to school.

Some kids at my school, especially the girls, are very superficial and outspoken about the clothes people wear. They have no problem dishing out insults and hurtful statements that are very embarrassing and humiliating, especially in front of other people. If we all wore uniforms, then maybe some of us could go through the day without criticism and ridiculing.

All in all, the teen years are difficult enough and could be made easier and more carefree, both at home and at school, with the endorsement of school uniforms. Even the job of the school administrators could be made a little easier if they didn't have to deal with dress code violations. Both young and old have pressures. Let's get rid of one of those pressures right now. Bring on the uniforms!

| Excellent = (5) | Good = (4) | Fair = (3) | Poor = (2) | Unsatisfactory = (1) |

Score	Characteristics of an Elaborated Essay
	Clearly stated main idea in the introduction
	Introduction, Body Paragraphs, Conclusion
	Two or three clearly stated supporting points or reasons
	Vivid examples/details/sensory images
	One elaborated paragraph with anecdote
	Smooth transition from paragraph to paragraph
	Satisfactory grammar, spelling, and punctuation
	Varied sentence structure
	Age appropriate vocabulary
	No sentences off-topic
	Total Score
	Final Score (total divided by 10)

Evaluate Elaborated Essays *(cont.)*

Topic: Uniforms

I think that school uniforms would be a great idea. First of all, you wouldn't have to worry about what you're going to wear that day. Rich kids can't make fun of other kids not wearing cool clothes. Third, you wouldn't get into trouble at school.

On school mornings I wake up and spend 15 minutes trying to decide what to wear to school. I know other kids spend longer. I live with my grandparents and this gets on Grandma's nerves. It's stressful for me too. If we wore uniforms, it would reduce time and arguments with your family. One morning last week, Grandma had to wait for me 20 minutes before I was ready to go. She got mad because it made me late to school. I got to school in a bad mood.

Next, some kids can't afford to buy new clothes or clothes that other kids consider cool. Like me, for instance: my grandma buys my clothes from low-budget stores. So people at school make fun of me which really hurts my feelings. They laugh behind our backs and talk about us. This wouldn't happen with uniforms.

My last reason is that you wouldn't get in trouble at school for being out of dress code. They wouldn't have to call your parents or give you a detention. I think that wearing uniforms to school is a great idea for the reasons I mentioned above.

Excellent = (5)	Good = (4)	Fair = (3)	Poor = (2)	Unsatisfactory = (1)

Score	Characteristics of an Elaborated Essay
	Clearly stated main idea in the introduction
	Introduction, Body Paragraphs, Conclusion
	Two or three clearly stated supporting points or reasons
	Vivid examples/details/sensory images
	One elaborated paragraph with anecdote
	Smooth transition from paragraph to paragraph
	Satisfactory grammar, spelling, and punctuation
	Varied sentence structure
	Age appropriate vocabulary
	No sentences off-topic
	Total Score
	Final Score (total divided by 10)

Evaluate Elaborated Essays *(cont.)*

Topic: Uniforms

I am very against wearing school uniforms. I don't think it's fair because this is a free country. We should always wear what we want and no one should take that away from us. It's enough that our parents are always taking away things and telling us what to do all the time. Different groups like different things to wear. My group likes baggy pants and long shirts. This shouldn't be taken away from us. It's not right. I don't want to wear dorky uniforms. Anyway, my dad can't afford uniforms and it's not fair to him to have to go out and spend more money. In my opinion this whole uniform idea should be thrown out. This is public school and not some private school.

Excellent = (5)	Good = (4)	Fair = (3)	Poor = (2)	Unsatisfactory = (1)

Score	Characteristics of an Elaborated Essay
	Clearly stated main idea in the introduction
	Introduction, Body Paragraphs, Conclusion
	Two or three clearly stated supporting points or reasons
	Vivid examples/details/sensory images
	One elaborated paragraph with anecdote
	Smooth transition from paragraph to paragraph
	Satisfactory grammar, spelling, and punctuation
	Varied sentence structure
	Age appropriate vocabulary
	No sentences off-topic
	Total Score
	Final Score (total divided by 10)

Evaluate Elaborated Essays *(cont.)*

Topic: Your local newspaper is looking for a student writer from every middle school in your area to report events in the students section. Write an essay convincing the editor that you should be selected to represent your school.

Nothing would please me more than to be on my way to becoming a famous journalist in my community. Working for your newspaper would provide the perfect opportunity to launch my career in this direction. Experience and dependability rate among my highest qualifications, and my commitment to excellence will prove that I am the perfect candidate for the job.

Most job openings seem to be advertising "Experience Needed" these days. Well, I have the kind of experience that I believe is required for this particular job. Having been voted unanimously as editor of our school newspaper for two years, I have always given 100% of my effort and have put in many after-school hours towards making our newspaper both interesting and exciting. As a matter of fact, our school paper is a huge success, and the increase in readership proves how much the students like reading it. In addition, receiving the "Best Editor" award last year further proves my dedication and commitment to writing. However, my proudest moment was when I was selected to be a writing tutor for our slow writers. One classmate, Jill, comes to mind when I think of this privilege. She was reported to have a difficult personality, and the teachers referred to her as a "resistant" learner. However, all of that changed when she started responding to my tutoring. Jill said that I made writing fun and easy for her. My reward for tutoring her came when she received an A on her essay about "What Freedom Means." The teacher even used her essay as a model for the rest of the class. I believe that helping Jill and others has made me a better writer.

Next, I would like to elaborate on my dependability. Finding someone who is dependable is sure to be a priority on any employer's list. I consider myself a very dependable student, daughter, and friend. Making straight A's and having perfect attendance are two goals that I have achieved while at my middle school. In addition, my parents can depend on me not only for excellent grades, but for also completing all assigned chores and responsibilities. However, I am especially proud of

Evaluate Elaborated Essays *(cont.)*

the fact that my friends can always depend on me for supporting them during difficult times and for supporting them in whatever they do. A quality you will consistently find in me is dependability. You can count on me to make sure that the news is reported and written accurately.

In conclusion, I would like to add that I take news reporting very seriously. I would be honored if I were the student chosen to represent our great school. My experience, my dependability, and especially my past and present performance as editor, make me a top choice, and one you won't regret.

P.S. I can furnish recommendations upon request.

Excellent = (5)	Good = (4)	Fair = (3)	Poor = (2)	Unsatisfactory = (1)

Score	Characteristic of Elaborated Essay
	Clearly stated main idea in the introduction
	Introduction, Body Paragraphs, Conclusion
	Two or three clearly stated supporting points or reasons
	Vivid examples/details/sensory images
	One elaborated paragraph with anecdote
	Smooth transition from paragraph to paragraph
	Satisfactory grammar, spelling, and punctuation
	Varied sentence structure
	Age appropriate vocabulary
	No sentences off topic
	Total Score
	Final Score (total divided by 10)

Evaluate Elaborated Essays *(cont.)*

<u>Topic</u>: Student Reporter

I believe you should pick me for a student reporter for the following reasons. I am very trustworthy and honest. I am also a very good writer.

First of all, I am a very trustworthy person. My parents say that I am the most trusting member of my family. They can trust me with anything. They can trust me with messages and watching the little kids. My grandma has me take care of her parrot when she goes out of town. I really like taking care of Petey and he likes me. My friends trust me too. They trust me with all of their secrets because they know I will never tell.

Second of all, I am an honest person. I have never lied to my family or my teachers or my friends. I always give honest answers to the police officer at my school and I will be honest with you. Honesty is the best policy. One time, someone in my homeroom stole the box of pennies we were collecting for a leukemia fundraiser. We all saw who did it. He was a bully and threatened to hurt us if we told. But, when I was asked, I told the truth.

Third of all, I am a very good writer. I get B's and C's on most of my writings. My teachers have always liked my writing. They said that I was very creative. I keep a journal at home where I write about everything that happens during the day. This gives me a lot of practice writing. I love to write and I will report all the news at my school whether it is good or bad. My reporting will be honest.

I'm the right person for the job. I will represent my school and all of the news. I am trustworthy, honest, and a good writer. So please pick me. Thank you.

Excellent = (5)	Good = (4)	Fair = (3)	Poor = (2)	Unsatisfactory = (1)

Score	Characteristics of an Elaborated Essay
	Clearly stated main idea in the introduction
	Introduction, Body Paragraphs, Conclusion
	Two or three clearly stated supporting points or reasons
	Vivid examples/details/sensory images
	One elaborated paragraph with anecdote
	Smooth transition from paragraph to paragraph
	Satisfactory grammar, spelling, and punctuation
	Varied sentence structure
	Age appropriate vocabulary
	No sentences off topic
	Total Score
	Final Score (total divided by 10)

Evaluate Elaborated Essays *(cont.)*

Topic: Student Reporter

I want very much to be a news reporter for my school. I have always wanted to do this, but was never picked for the school newspaper. I guess the teacher didn't like me. I have been picked for other things though. I was picked to collect papers and wash the boards every day. One year I was picked to take messages to the front office. Anyway, I can get the news from my school and then write it down for you every week. I can get my dad to take me to your office to deliver it to you. I will make sure that it is typed and very neat. I have a great typewriter in my room that I got for my birthday. My teacher said I have a very pretty handwriting which is very important when you want me to write things instead of type them.

I will never let you down. When I start something I finish it no matter what. Some kids like to go out and talk on the phone all the time. I do not do this because I will come home and write for you. I don't even watch television or have pets. So I will have lots of time for everything you want me to do. You will be proud of me. My parents are proud of me too. I leave them notes whenever I get on my bike and go somewhere so they don't have to worry. I always go on errands for my mom when she is sick. When my little sister needs milk I go to the convenient store to get it. I can do anything you ask me to do.

I really deserve this job because I will be good at it. Don't you think I will too?

| Excellent = (5) | Good = (4) | Fair = (3) | Poor = (2) | Unsatisfactory = (1) |

Score	Characteristics of an Elaborated Essay
	Clearly stated main idea in the introduction
	Introduction, Body Paragraphs, Conclusion
	Two or three clearly stated supporting points or reasons
	Vivid examples/details/sensory images
	One elaborated paragraph with anecdote
	Smooth transition from paragraph to paragraph
	Satisfactory grammar, spelling, and punctuation
	Varied sentence structure
	Age appropriate vocabulary
	No sentences off topic
	Total Score
	Final Score (total divided by 10)

Tips for Writing an Expository Essay

❏ Clearly state the main idea (what you are explaining) in the introduction and make your paper inviting to read.

❏ Include supporting points.

❏ Include examples and details that support each point.

❏ Include vivid adjectives, strong verbs, and exact nouns.

❏ Include quotes and/or dialogue to make your paper interesting.

❏ Use sensory language when appropriate.

❏ Use transitional words when moving from paragraph to paragraph.

❏ Stay focused; no sentence should be off-topic.

❏ Arrange sentences in a logical order and vary their structure by changing the way the sentences begin. See pages 52–53 for examples.

❏ Make your conclusion clear to show that you have finished; don't leave the reader hanging.

Remember to always keep in mind who your audience will be. Consider how much or how little they know about your topic, and provide details accordingly.

Tips for Writing a Persuasive Essay

- ❏ Clearly state your opinion about the issue in the introduction.

- ❏ Include reasons which support your opinion.

- ❏ Support each reason with examples and details; include facts and/or statistics whenever you can.

- ❏ Compare or contrast some of your details whenever you can.

- ❏ Include an anecdote that strongly supports one of your points.

- ❏ Quote an important source, like an expert, an article in a magazine or newspaper, or a book, to strengthen your position.

- ❏ Include vivid adjectives, strong verbs, and exact nouns.

- ❏ Use sensory language and transitional words when moving from paragraph to paragraph.

- ❏ Stay focused, vary your sentence structure, and make sure all sentences relate to your topic.

- ❏ In your conclusion, offer suggestions for solutions or actions that can be taken in the future.

Remember to always keep in mind who your audience will be. Consider which side of your argument they will be on, and adjust your essay accordingly to address their concerns or sympathies.

Writing Elaborated Essays

Directions: Now it is your turn to write elaborated essays of your own. Below are some suggested topics for practice. A blank web list has been provided on the next page. Remember to refer to the list of characteristics on page 63, and don't forget to use elaboration techniques.

Suggested Topics

Topic: Many of us have wondered what it would be like to trade places with someone for a day. Explain in an essay with whom you would like to trade places.

Topic: During the school year, most students have a favorite class. Describe your favorite class in an essay.

Topic: One of your best friends wants to drop out of school. Write an essay convincing him/her that he/she should remain in school.

Topic: You would like to be considered as a writer for your school newspaper. Write an essay convincing your teacher that you should be selected.

Topic: You would like to have a raise in your allowance. Write an essay convincing your parents that this raise is necessary.

Topic: Many students at your middle school believe that they don't have enough time in-between classes. Write an essay telling your principal whether you agree or disagree with this statement.

Topic: Many students at your middle school dislike the cafeteria lunches. Write an essay explaining why you agree or disagree with this.

Topic: Your neighbor is looking for a pet sitter for her dog and two cats. Write an essay convincing her that you are the right person for the job.

Creating a Web List for Your Essay

Web List Diagram

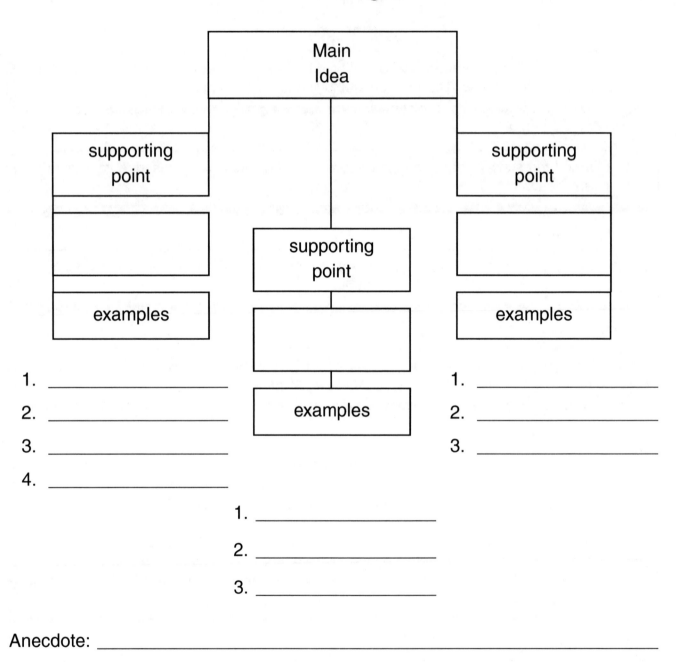

Main
Idea

supporting
point

supporting
point

supporting
point

examples

examples

examples

1. _____
2. _____
3. _____
4. _____

1. _____
2. _____
3. _____

1. _____
2. _____
3. _____

Anecdote: _____

© Teacher Created Resources, Inc.

Answer Key

Page 9

1. spin, twist, twirl
2. glimpse, observe, stare
3. race, dash, hurry
4. crawl, limp, strut
5. roam, drift, meander
6. declare, reply, respond
7. gorge, devour, consume
8. create, design, construct
9. offer, present, furnish
10. leave, depart, withdraw
11. locate, discover, detect
12. desire, wish, crave

Page 10

1. clip, tear, snip
2. gulp, sip, swallow
3. obtain, possess, pull
4. place, hand, arrange
5. grab, acquire, snatch
6. quiz, inquire, question
7. cackle, giggle, chuckle
8. contemplate, believe, imagine
9. operate, utilize, employ
10. store, preserve, conserve

Page 11–Answers may vary.

1. raced
2. imagine
3. arranged
4. located
5. constructed
6. declared
7. stored
8. clipped
9. obtained
10. crawled
11. won
12. laughed at
13. contemplated
14. grabbed
15. depart

Page 14

1. trustworthy/dependable
2. miniature
3. considerate
4. mischievous
5. giant, enormous
6. popular
7. steep
8. battered
9. hilarious
10. interesting
11. dedicated
12. exciting
13. generous
14. delicate
15. unforgivable
16. enormous, giant
17. dependable, trustworthy
18. devastating
19. graceful
20. towering

Page 15

1. noisy, muddy
2. well-lit or shadowy, loud
3. closely-knit, annual
4. dark, narrow
5. crowded
6. experienced, frightened
7. excited, anxious
8. well-built, solid
9. flowered
10. older, messy
11. long
12. fire, high

Page 16

1. fun-loving
2. wonderful
3. sweet-toothed
4. delicious
5. pink
6. yummy
7. chocolate
8. concession
9. cheesy
10. greasy
11. tasty

Answer Key (cont.)

Page 16 (Cont.)

12. thrilling
13. exhilarating
14. daring
15. adventurous
16. exciting
17. wild
18. challenging
19. midway
20. video
21. cultural
22. magnificent
23. horse
24. talented
25. graceful
26. entertaining

Page 17

1. American
2. serious
3. peer
4. uncomfortable
5. influential
6. popular
7. disrespectful
8. safety
9. tempting
10. dangerous
11. potent
12. alcoholic
13. illegal
14. insurmountable
15. awesome
16. perfect
17. extracurricular
18. art
19. continuous
20. mental
21. physical
22. stomach
23. emotional
24. social

Page 20

1. ice cream
2. events
3. vegetables

4. careers
5. locations
6. spacecraft
7. chairs
8. boats
9. sports
10. organs
11. snakes
12. rides
13. appliances
14. guns
15. dogs
16. religions
17. clergy
18. decorations
19. hobbies
20. references

Pages 21-24—Answers will vary.

Page 26—Answers will vary.

Pages 28-29

1. dream car; stylish clothes, comfortable and luxurious home
2. lower rates of cancer and heart disease; maintain weight within healthy range; better blood pressure and cholesterol count
3. death from lung cancer and other related diseases; smokers cough; shortness of breath during exercise
4. feeds and shelters stray animals; cooks for homeless; contributes to charity
5. sour milk; stale bread; bugs in cereal
6. family members can bird watch, hike, toast marshmallows at campfire
7. snow skiing; snowboarding; ice skating; snowshoeing; sledding
8. cayenne and red pepper; chili powder; jalapeno pepper; green chiles
9. chicken soup; comfortable bed/warm coverings; plays games
10. celery/carrot sticks; lettuce with fat-free dressing; fruits/green vegetables

Pages 30-32–answers will vary

Page 34–Paragraph A

Page 35

1. I believe that I am very responsible for my age.
2. responsibility

Answer Key *(cont.)*

Page 35 *(Cont.)*

3. clean clothes; babysit little sister; prepare dinner; Saturday babysitting; Saturday work at Dad's office

4. Beginning—One time I forgot to . . .

   Middle—so he made me . . .

   End—I made sure . . .

5. humiliated; ashamed

6. All of these responsibilities . . .

Pages 36-38–Answers will vary.

Page 39

2. warm, sunny, splashed
3. sweet, sticky, exciting
4. aroma, greasy
5. clammy, faster and faster
6. sour, sweet, salty
7. old, torn, scruffy, missing
8. beat, stomped
9. cold, bleak, gloomy
10. grasped, clutched, hugged

Page 40

First paragraph:

stomped—sight

slippery—touch

narrow—sight

blistering—touch

collapsed—touch

stale—taste

humid—touch

black leather—sight

sticky—touch

shouted, yelled, laughed—sound

crowded—touch

grape-flavored—taste, smell

growled—sound

chocolate-chip brownies—taste

pressed—touch

squeaky—sound

dashed—sight

Second paragraph:

hard—touch

wooden—sight

yelled—sound

cheered—sound

salty peanuts—taste

thick—touch

sweet—taste

chocolate—taste

buttery—taste

popcorn—taste

greasy—sight, touch

pizza—taste

hollered—sound

high-five—touch

shivered—touch

sun—sight

call—sound

screamed—sound

cheered—sound

Page 41

1. moist	16. soft
2. moss	17. mushy
3. rich dirt	18. slippery
4. white	19. rippling
5. fluffy	20. rustling
6. towering	21. curving
7. thickly	22. sweet
8. canopy	23. fresh
9. thin streams	24. clammy
10. push	25. thumped
11. pointed	26. croaking
12. round	27. red
13. greens	28. yellow
14. browns	29. neon
15. yellows	30. hopped

Pages 42-44–Answers will vary.

Page 46

The anecdote begins with, "Last year, our school sent..." and ends with, "wouldn't mind wearing a uniform to work myself."

The anecdote begins with, "I remember just two weeks ago..." and ends with, "that really made her feel special."

Pages 47–Answers will vary.

Page 48

1. mother—genie
2. hands—butterflies
3. people—ants
4. I—jackrabbit
5. words—boomerang

Answer Key (cont.)

Page 48 (*Cont.*)

6. she—dog
7. self-esteem—steel
8. I—thunderbolt
9. he—person who has just won the lottery
10. I—pearl in an oyster

Page 49

Paragraph 1 – Tony is like a heartless, brutal machine

Paragraph 2 – You'll come out purring like a kitten

Page 50

A. Over 58,000 Americans died; 300,000 wounded or disabled

B. 1970—8% were over 65 years old; 1990 – 12% were over 65 years old

   2000—20% over 65 years old

C. Over two million teens suffer from depression; 40% seek medical or professional help, Nearly 75% who do receive treatment do not recover

Page 51

Paragraph 1—$20.00 per week on food; $200–$500 annual visits to vet; $15.00 per month for vitamins; $35.00 per month for stable; $30.00–$40.00 for training lessons

Paragraph 2—discovery of steroids in 20th century by Germans in WWII; U.S. weight lifters used steroids in the 1950s; 2–11 percent of high school athletes, 10–20 percent of college athletes, 50–90 percent of amateur body builders use steroids; educational programs developed in U.S. in the 1980s.

Page 58

Suggested score—1.4

Page 59

Suggested score—2.9

Page 60

Suggested score—5.0

Pages 68–78

Answers will vary

Page 82

vivid verbs—wander, drowned, meander, nurture, wrestle

vivid adjectives—dependable, lovable, ideal, chocolate chip, school-aged, careful, two-year-old, non-stop, irresponsible, devoted, lovable, difficult, loving

examples that support dependability—do necessary chores: feed, bathe, and help kids with homework; not open doors to strangers, no friends over, no unsupervised outside play.

examples that support devoted and lovable—play favorite games and puzzles, wrestle, "Barbies"

anecdote—"Not too long ago. . . would have never reached Stacey in time to rescue her."

quotes/dialogue—First paragraph: "Dependable" "lovable"

similes—People tell me I'm as devoted as a dog

sensory words/images—chocolate, barking, wrestle

facts/statistics—2000 American children a year drown

Page 84

vivid verbs—falling, unstrapped, slipping, slamming, challenged, grabbed, flipped, turned, twisted, yelling

vivid adjectives—exhilarating, dangerous, powerful, loud, wild, sharp, thrilling, challenging, brisk, plunging, narrow, steep

examples that support fear of riding roller coasters—not ride them on field trips, feared falling out, becoming unstrapped, something going wrong with engine, slamming into ground

examples supporting that riding roller coasters is fun—wild loops, sharp turns, high speeds, brisk wind on face, plunging dips, flipped over

anecdote—"One day in 6th grade . . . I found myself waiting in line again."

quotes/dialogue—"Erika, I'll ride it by myself." "Let's ride it again!"

similes—I feel like I am master of the universe…

sensory words/images—falling out, becoming unstrapped, slipping off narrow and steep track, slamming into ground, brisk wind, plunging dip, upside down, turned and twisted, yelling

facts/statistics—60, 70, 80 mile-per-hour speeds

Page 97

Suggested score—5.0

Page 99

Suggested score—3.0

Page 100

Suggested score—1.2

Page 102

Suggested Score—5.0

Page 103

Suggested Score—3.5

Page 104

Suggested Score—1.5